To my brother
Mark

Much love,
William

MISADVENTURES IN HOSPITALITY

William Wallen

authorHOUSE®

AuthorHouse™
1663 Liberty Drive
Bloomington, IN 47403
www.authorhouse.com
Phone: 1 (800) 839-8640

Published by AuthorHouse 07/20/2018

ISBN: 978-1-5462-5143-9 (sc)
ISBN: 978-1-5462-5142-2 (hc)
ISBN: 978-1-5462-5141-5 (e)

Library of Congress Control Number: 2018908580

Print information available on the last page.

CONTENTS

This book is dedicated to Terry Crews and everyone who works in or has worked in the industry of hospitality... Except for you... You know who you are....

INTRODUCTION

"Man is least himself when he talks in his own person. Give him a mask, and he will tell you the truth."
-Oscar Wilde

You're probably never going to read this because no one ever seems to read the introduction. So, of course, I decided to bury all the treasure-finding clues that will help you figure out the rest of the book. You're welcome.

People have always said that strange and interesting stories seem to just find me like I have some sort of gravitational pull that just draws them into my life experience.

Which is exactly why, when I was in the fifth grade, a cannibal child molester stole my kickball.

I'm not joking about the cannibal child molester. To be fair, and even more importantly, the kickball wasn't mine personally. It did in fact belong to our fifth-grade classroom. But I can assure you that the following deeds did indeed transpire.

A bunch of us were outside at recess playing this variation of dodgeball that we had made up. Rules, like etiquette in front of your female classmates, were merely a suggestion. Anyways, the ball ended up going over the fence and out in the street. Just when we were going to ask the recess aide to grab it for us, a red car pulls up and stops right next to it.

The door opens, and a man puts his legs out of the vehicle and reaches down and grabs a hold of the ball. He proceeds to pause for a moment. We are all waving our arms in the air wanting him to just throw it back. Then he suddenly just grabs it, gets fully back into his car, and just speeds off like the piece of shit he is.

A few months later, a known sex offender was brought up on several charges of molestation, rape, and cannibalism, and upon seeing his face on T.V. I remember all I could think was, "That's the guy! That's him!"

Oh, wow you really are reading this. Let me see if I can find a way to tie this into my book here.

I guess you could say this is just one example of the strange experiences I have encountered throughout my life. Although it was this experience that lead me to believe that I could not be surprised by anything anymore. As soon as I started working in hospitality I was proven wrong. And every single time that I thought I was pressed firmly against the Willy Wonka Glass Elevator of Possibilities, some fellow primate would graciously shed their stupidity or insanity that would prove me wrong. Oh, so wrong.

I like to think that working in such an industry as hospitality makes you a better person. Simply because it shows you exactly who and what you do not want to be, and you find yourself striving to be better.

Hotels are an Oscar-Wilde-like mask with concrete walls and neatly-wrapped soap...under this mask, the swarms of humanity acted out who they really were. And I was their audience.

It has been said that we tell stories to make sense of what happened. This is very fitting for me here. I find myself continuously trying to make sense of the events that transpired and continue to transpire across check-in desks in every state in America, and around the globe. (Unless you're a Flat Earther, then this would be across the entire square thing. You're also wrong.)

I am presenting to you a collection of stories that is full of all kinds of vitriol. It is very real and raw and could possibly even offend some. I have changed the names of people involved and possible locations were changed or omitted. Otherwise though, these stories remain completely truthful.

One brief, but again truthful, account was something that happened a few months after my four-year mark in hospitality. I was in no way new to all the happenings of this industry. I was very well seasoned, and one could say a bit salty at times (pardon the pun).

Here's an aperitif of what you might sample on the silver tray of a daily shift in my hotel:

There was a brief prank phone call I had one late night. Between the prank calls I would get at work and the ones I made as a kid empowered me to deal with these creatively.

It was late into a night audit shift. That means we spent an entire shift writing down various numbers and watching Netflix, not necessarily in that order. Like a flare in the ocean, suddenly the phone rang out of nowhere. It was a small group of kids - probably pre-teens, full of pre-crushed dreams and Hannah Montana monologues, possibly early teens making prank calls.

This prank caller said, "Uhhhh yeah, this is your customer in room 129 and uhhhh we got some people banging on the door and being loud."

We did not have a room 129. Not to mention this was obviously a kid trying to make his voice sound unnecessarily deeper. This being tied to the fact that I could see on the caller ID that he was calling from a phone line outside the hotel and I could hear his little friends snickering in the background.

I was tired and ready to go home. I really did not want to deal with a prank call right at that moment. So, I responded how I felt would be the best way to turn the tables of pranking around on them.

I said, "You know your parents don't love you and took off in the middle of the night, so they wouldn't have to see you, again right?"

There was a bit of a pause before he gave me a bit of a disturbed sounding response of, "Wha... Wha... What?"

He sounded almost like he was holding back tears.

To which I said, "Go ahead and check. I'll wait."

Having the attributes of being snarky, irreverent became a necessity of carrying out this job.

If you're still reading this then you probably have a sense of humor that is just as disturbed enough as mine to enjoy this book, so I guess I'll just sort of end this introduction and let you get on with it.

Enjoy.

HOW THE HOTEL INDUSTRY
GRABBED ME BY THE BALLS

When I was a child I would tell my mother that I wanted to be a bodybuilder, actor, wizard, entrepreneur, rich guy. But only in the hotel business could one become these things… Or interact with the strange side of humanity that was these things and more.

While I was in my early 20's I had moved out of state for a little while, and by a series of events ended up returning to my hometown.

After returning I was in obvious need of a job. I recall the day I was hanging out with a friend of mine from high school named Morgan. We were hanging out and catching up. She had, a few months prior, been hired to do night audit.

Among our reminiscing, she told me this story about a recent ordeal. It was a tale where she suffered at the hands of a 16-year-old girl while working one night. For our purposes today, we will call this girl Mildred. I really don't know what her real name is, but I feel like Mildred is somehow fitting.

So, Morgan was standing at the desk that fateful evening. She was just working and minding her own business when this girl walked up to her at the desk.

Morgan had her head down and didn't hear this girl walk up. She happened to look up and upon making eye contact with this girl, the girl said to Morgan, "Hey! You wanna fight?"

"What?" Morgan said being rather taken back by this question.

"Do you wanna fight?!" The Mildred repeated.

"What?! No! Go away!" Morgan replied before continuing to attempt to get her work done for the night.

That was when the real fun began. This girl grabs the lamp that was on the desk and hits Morgan on the head with it.

"Oh my God! What the fuck?! You fucking dumb bitch!" Morgan exclaimed after being struck by the lamp before continuing with death threats and all sorts of vitriol.

This Mildred girl got freaked out not expecting Morgan to have any sort of reaction. Which I know is very strange. I mean, she hit someone in the head with a fucking lamp. What did she think was going to happen? But then again, the intelligence of this girl is questionable. She did after all try to start a fight with a random person and then was surprised when said person began threatening her life upon being assaulted with a lamp.

Who the hell assaults someone with a lamp anyway? I am aware that this incident occurred in a hotel and the number of blunt objects is limited, but a lamp? Really? Beside that this is now aggravated assault. Had she just punched Morgan this would have been bad enough, but now this has become a felony and who wants to be sitting in jail and having to explain that they are in for hitting someone with a lamp?

Morgan called the police. Being as Mildred was a minor her parents were brought to the desk to deal with this wonderful incident as well. I imagine they were super happy with her. They probably were named Hank and Kathy and I am sure they took her out for ice cream to celebrate her newest life achievement.

No charges were pressed against this girl, but she did have to pay for the lamp.

I really am not sure the reason behind not pressing charges. I don't know if they came to some agreement on top of the payment for the lamp or what. Morgan did say, and I quote, "My blood lust was untethered, and my rage knew no bounds. I wanted vengeance." She is quite the colorful character.

Even after hearing this story… Call it being naive to the fact that such incidences are not uncommon in this industry, call it my desperate need for income, or maybe it was a bit of both… I had to open my big mouth and ask Morgan if her workplace was hiring. And sure, as hell they were, and she even drove me down to the hotel to pick up an application.

I applied and the next day got a call for an interview for the day after. Within 48 hours of grabbing the application an interview would happen.

I remember during the interview I felt very confident. At one point I was asked how I felt about people which I said, "I love people! People are great!" I really wasn't lying. I used to enjoy people. Then overtime my I developed a deep seeded misanthropy.

Everything was moving very quickly and to me it seemed like I had a light at the end of the tunnel. Then the next day after my interview I got a phone call offering me the job which I accepted.

That day I opened a new chapter in my life.

I want to make this clear that I worked in a hotel not a motel. There is a difference. A hotel is the nice place you stay at on vacation where as a motel is the kind of place where every room has a meth lab and just walking in the lobby you will probably get hepatitis. One of the best descriptions I have heard to differentiate between the two was that a hotel is where you got to sleep with prostitutes where as a motel is where you go to murder prostitutes.

Like most people, I had worked in customer service jobs before. I also spent a good amount of time in sales too. Working in hospitality is a bit of both except predicting the future with whom you are going to encounter and what sort of headache they will bring you. I learned very quickly that you will meet all the walks of life. All the good, the bad, and the ugly... especially the bad and ugly ones.

When I worked customer service jobs I complained all the time about the horrible customers we would get. But none of them held a candle to the guests I would deal with. The level of absurdity that they would bring (and continue to bring to all of those working in this industry) remains unmatched.

I want to make it very clear that this is not meant to be me complaining. This whole book is an expose' of the more memorable crazy experiences laid out in print for all of you to enjoy at my expense.

The accounts following this chapter are all true. Sit back and relish in the misery of others.

GLUTEN FREE LADY

My early career was punctuated by random episodes of finding myself at the front desk on various Friday mornings. One time, my general manager was up front with me. And it was just him. Just us. Two amigos. Yeah. Allow me to paint a picture of my place of employment:

My general manager, Jim, tunneled in and out of his office all day like an inexperienced drug mule. But I guess that was part of the job: a slave to the harsh yelps of customers and the red-black ink dance that splatters itself across our monthly reports. I got it. I just didn't like it.

I recall that morning well. I was wearing my uniform blue button up shirt, black slacks, and of course dress shoes. I looked like a total douche.

If hotels were ships, I was glued to my own special little perch, my own sphere of command: the left side of the desk that day. If you were standing on the opposite side of the desk than I do, then I would be on the right side of the desk. The other side was also closer to Jim's office which made it easier for him to pop out and help if need be.

So that morning was busy. Just full of traffic. Even for a morning coming off a sold-out night it was busy. I had a lobby full of people. Seating in the breakfast bar was full when I had arrived that morning but was slowly tapering off. There were just people coming and going all morning.

Thankfully so I did not have a continuous flow of asshole guests to deal with. Such times do come upon us, but this day was not one of them. I will say though that the assholes I dealt with that day... The crazy psycho bitch lady and her shitbag husband were the equivalent of a constant flow of bullshit to deal with at work. So, I suppose really in all honesty the only thing to be thankful for is the fact that I can share this tale with all you readers out there.

I promise you that this story is completely true. This shit totally happened. At the time it was one of the stranger and rather annoying experiences of my life. However, I now can look back upon it fondly as it was indeed entertaining.

Here is what took place that day...

I was just standing there working. You know simple shit. I would answer the phone, check guests out, help people find the freeway, look up the weather report for them, and in general just used my acting skills to make everyone I spoke to feel like I give a shit about them.

Then it happened. This woman, who will forever be known as Gluten Free Lady, walks up to me at the desk holding a Styrofoam plate and a banana.

She must have been in her early to mid to late 60's. She was wearing a light blue blouse and khakis. But not just any khakis. They were like the perfect pair of old people khakis. You know the kind of khakis you see older people wearing and the only explanation for this is that every senior citizen shop at the same goddamn store? They are the kind of pants one wears when they have given up on life. She was wearing those. So, I knew this was not going to go well for anyone.

This woman walks up to me and asks me, "Um, excuse me... Is there ANYTHING over in the breakfast area that is gluten free? I have a gluten intolerance." In a rather snobby tone.

I proceeded to name off everything we offered for breakfast that was indeed gluten free, which was a good 75% of the fucking food over in the breakfast bar. And I did this while remaining to be very polite to her.

None of what I had said was in anyway what she wanted to hear. Gluten Free Lady was one of those people who is never fully satisfied with anything. She also wanted me to tell her something we had that not only was gluten free but something she enjoyed eating. I guess I'm supposed to be a fucking mind reader or something to be able to correctly guess what she would enjoy in this criterion and some sort of wizard where I could conjure all her heart's desires out of thin air.

After I exhausted every little thing we had to offer her she finally just said, "Oh great. There's nothing. I guess I will have to settle for a banana."

Just then her husband walked up. He was basically dressed like Mister Rogers except he was wearing polished loafers and not chucks. He also was not nearly as cool as Mister Rogers. This guy was a giant sack of shit. Mister Rogers on the other hand is one badass motherfucker.

This douche nozzle walks up next to her staring me down like he thought he could set me on fire with his mind like he was in a Stephen King story or something. He just walks up to me with a death glare, stands next to her and asks, "Is everything okay dear?" All the while staring at me like he wants me to die some horrible death.

She went into detail telling him about the heartache the hotel and I especially have caused her. He just says, "Well at least you have your banana waiting for you. I'll go get the rest of our things while you eat." He then proceeds to walk away back up to their room.

Across the lobby from the desk there stood a fireplace that blocks the view of the middle part of the breakfast bar seating area. Gluten Free Lady walks behind the fireplace and sits down. Which then created a blind spot in which I could not see Gluten Free Lady.

I had to see what exactly she was doing as morbid curiosity dictates. I just could not believe she would be eating with all the fuss she made. So, I moved to the side a bit to get a better view of her. I saw her just sitting there with her unpeeled banana on her plate while she looked around with a sad look on her face like a kid her lost their mom in Walmart.

I took it upon myself to forewarn Jim about my dealings with her because I had a feeling this was going to turn into an issue of epic proportion. And as luck would have it she walks her sad ass back up to the desk for some more groaning about the supposed lack of gluten free items for breakfast.

She comes up and asks if my manager is around, so she may speak with him. Jim hears this and walks out.

Gluten Free Lady just goes off on this rant about how she has a gluten allergy and how we should be more open to the idea of providing more gluten free options on the menu. She just went off for a while about this shit and then expected Jim to be able to give her an answer that she wanted.

Jim basically just gave her the answers I gave her. I was especially fond of when Jim said to her, "We have eggs. Those are gluten free." And this suggestion was not good enough for her because, and I fucking quote, "No. No I can't have eggs either. If it's not cooked right, then I just can't stand the taste and I'm pretty sure it makes me break out."

After this small feeling of defeat Gluten Free Lady then goes back to her seat to resume sulking and staring at her banana some more.

Jim and I went into his office where he just told me not to worry much about her. He just explained that people like her just want attention and just want to constantly bitch. Which is true. All this woman ultimately wanted was to be unhappy. She is just one of those shitbag people who only ever wants to be fucking miserable.

Then it happened... All her bullshit began to come to a head...

I go back out front to find her standing there wanting to yell some more at my general manager and I about everything. On the verge of tears her rant went a little something like this:

"I just don't understand why your company cannot provide a service for its guests like me who have a SEVERE allergy to gluten! You claim to be family friendly, but you won't take into consideration my feelings!"

There was really very little more Jim could do for her at this point. He tried making food suggestions again. Among his suggestions she had to escalate the situation even more. Somehow, among his suggestions, she also has now developed an allergy to dairy. None of his suggestions were anything new, but she had to go on a rant about her dairy allergy as well as her gluten allergy. Due to how abrupt that one came about, I can only assume it was an allergy that she developed in the short time we were speaking with her.

She just interrupted Jim and said, "Excuse me! I just told you I have a severe gluten allergy! And now not, not only are you refusing to rectify the situation for me but now you are suggesting that I consume a product containing dairy?! What is wrong with you?! Why don't you know I am lactose intolerant?!" At this point she began to tear up. Her husband still nowhere to be found. Either he was slow at packing their bags or was trying to hang himself.

"What about me?!" Gluten Free Lady cried as she pounded her chest.

"Would you like me to go somewhere and get you something?" Jim said.

She continued to cry as she said to Jim, "No! That's not good enough!"

Gluten Free Lady goes and sits back down at her chair and begins to eat her banana while crying. Have you ever seen a 65-year-old woman eat a banana while crying? I have... It's hilarious.

Jim turned towards me cringing trying to hold back laughter. He sorts of slightly motions with his hand while nodding his head to the side to signal me to go into his office with him.

As soon as he shut the door we began to laugh so hard we were in tears. But who wouldn't be? This lady is out of her fucking mind! Of course, to make matters more humorous for us Jim zoomed in the security camera in the breakfast bar, so it was focused right in on this lady crying while eating a banana. It was the funniest fucking thing I had seen in a long time. I laughed so hard I nearly shit myself.

When she finished chewing on her banana and wiped her tears we had to look alive. She began to approach the desk once again. I decided to try and give my boss a break and go out there first.

Full knowing what was about to transpire I still had to ask her, "How can I help you ma'am?"

Before responding verbally, she first gave me a very over the top scowl. After a moment she said she needed to speak with my manager. He then came out to speak with her or rather stand there and be yelled at. I moved back to the other side of the desk to help anyone else who would happen to come by while still listening to what she was saying.

Jim asks how he can help her and she managed to step it up a notch by starting the crying once again and saying, "Why can't your company look out for me?! What about me?! I have traveled ALL ACROSS THE COUNTRY! I have read reviews online! Many hotels now have a gluten free menu for those of us with a gluten intolerance! I have seen these reviews! They say things like 'Nice stay. Has gluten free food.' I have never been treated so unfairly! WHAT ABOUT ME?!"

All that Jim knew to do was offer once again to leave the hotel and buy her something from anywhere she likes. She is not paying for it. The hotel is. He is saying that he will take money from the register and go buy her whatever the hell she wants to eat for breakfast.

Gluten Free Lady just gave him a look of disgust like she was just called every insult in the book and looked at him and said, "No! NOOOO!!! That just isn't good enough! Too little too late! Don't you understand that there are grocery stores with whole aisles filled with food just for people like me! Why don't you care about what is going on?! What about me?!"

All I could think was, "Yeah I get it lady. You have a food allergy, but it still is not my fault that nature wants you dead."

"Look I'm really sorry. I would still happily go get you something if you wanted." Jim said when he got a moment's break from her screeching.

She grew angrier and decided to add some spice to her story. Her husband had also walked back up at this time. I guess he didn't hang himself after all. Oh well better luck next time I guess. She looked Jim dead in the face and said, "Look I told you that it's too little too late! And I will have you know that last night I had some rice cakes to eat because I can't have gluten. I wanted some peanut butter to put on them. I came to the desk and ask your employee over there for some peanut butter. He threw the pen out of his hand and SLAMMED on the desk and said, 'If you want peanut butter then you can go to the store and buy some peanut butter your own God damn self!' I couldn't believe what I was seeing!"

And I cannot believe it either. So somehow the night prior when I wasn't even there... I snapped on this lady when she asked me for some peanut butter and did so in such a way that could have caused me to lose my job... Right... I'm sure that happened.

Jim just looked at me with the most confused look imaginable. I just shrugged and put my hands up.

It was about this time that Gluten Free Lady's husband looked over at me to once again give me his glare. I really don't know what was up with that. Maybe he was hot for me or something. Who knows? But I digress, he comes over to me and lets out this rather long sigh. I can only imagine that he had an enlarged prostate and this sigh he let out of was a sigh of relief as he let out an epic piss he had been holding in due to his prostate issues but it's cool because he was wearing adult diapers and it had been a while since he had eaten asparagus, so no one is going to smell the piss... It was that kind of sigh if you can imagine.

After he was finished with his sigh he handed me his room keys. He then said to me, "Checking out... The stay could have been better. First of all, my wife has severe food allergies..."

I quickly interjected by saying, "Yes. She has made this abundantly clear all morning."

Her husband once again gave me his glare. He continued, "As I was saying. My wife has severe food allergies. We went out to dinner and where we went had mostly things on the menu that she could not eat. All my wife could eat there was a salad. My wife had a salad for dinner."

Again, I had to interject, "Well if that's the case then why didn't you just decide to leave and go somewhere else where she could eat something more substantial?"

I gathered this did not sit very well with him as once again I got the glare.

"As I was saying." He said, "After our terrible time at dinner... My wife asked you for peanut butter and you refused her peanut butter."

At this point in the morning I was beyond done with dealing with these assholes. All I could think to say was, "Yeah I have a tendency to do that."

He wrapped up our conversation by saying, "We will not be coming back."

This was so heartbreaking to hear. This crazy lady and her Mister Rogers wanna be husband who was not even a fraction as cool are telling me that they will never stay at my hotel again.

He carried their bags out with his head down. While she remained very animated and crying and screaming the whole way out the door.

Jim and I took a moment to go to his office and laugh and re-watch some of the footage of this woman crying while eating a banana.

TRAVELCON PHONE CALL

Many people enjoy using third party internet sites for their booking needs. I for one am not one of these people, because I tend to live my life untroubled by a constant coat of garbage coming at me through the computer. Let me explain.

I like that such websites exist to drive up hotel revenue across the world, create jobs, and give guests an ease of booking. But I hate how many problems can often cause issues for both the guest as well as the property.

It is for this reason that those of us in this line of work suggest that you book online directly through the hotel's website and not a third-party site. I mean they have a lot of benefits too, but I do not personally suggest them first thing.

Third party sites are like clumsy butlers that pour caviar in your champagne glass and serve you a plate of wine. For example, I do not know how many times people have been booked in for the wrong dates or even the wrong property.

When I say that they often book a guest at the wrong property I do not mean that they are attempting to be malicious in anyway (like how Jeeves is just a little on the spectrum, but we straighten his tie and tell him he's doing a great job and can't fire him because he's Great Aunt Bethany's spoiled little nephew). What I am saying is that they literally, occasionally, will not know what hotel they are booking on.

You are probably wondering how this could be as any sane person would. Well allow me to share a personal experience that became literally one for the book:

I was minding my own business working the evening shift at my hotel. Was all in uniform with my button up shirt, slacks, and handy little name tag I wear so people knew I was a sentient being with a name they could call me besides "Hey you" or "ass-face." (However, if you see a Jehovah's Witness or something with those name tags throwing a Bible at your front door with a smile, please feel free to use those names). I was supposed to look professional but just looked and felt like a total dumbass. But hey at least I know who I am! I have a name tag! Retaining such lucidity about who I am and where I am came in handy for what was about to transpire.

The phone had not rung for some time. This was in no way disappointing. A night free of commotion was always best.

Filling my evening with various social media outlets and stupid videos; I was feeling good about the remainder of my evening while being realistic that someone or something could totally ruin this winning streak I was having that day.

Suddenly, the phone rang for the first time in at least an hour. I looked over and glared at the phone in irritation before answering. Who could be disturbing my quiet evening?

I answered the phone hoping this would be a quick call from someone asking me if we had a pool or something.

Upon answering I go through our brand standard opening greeting like I always do.

In return I was greeted by a man's voice saying, "Hi this is Steve with Travelcon."

"Hi Steve. What can I do for you this evening?" I said.

Steve continued, "Well I was just calling to confirm that this was indeed the Relaxation Inn."

Had dipshit here listened to me when I answered he would already have the answer to this. Which is no… This is NOT the Relaxation Inn. I figured for once I would be nice and allow this guy to save face.

I went on to correct him, "Actually no sir. This is not the Relaxation Inn."

Before I was able to ask if he wanted the correct number to the Relaxation Inn, Steve chimes in like a spoiled teenager with a new Instagram account, "Well I have this number listed as the Relaxation Inn."

I was slightly annoyed but ultimately this was just a minor inconvenience at this point.

Repeating myself from earlier, "This is not the Relaxation Inn."

Steve continued with his stuck-up attitude and said back like a broken record, "Well, this number is listed on my records as being the Relaxation Inn."

This was starting to get more annoying. I really do not see what is hard to understand about this. His records are showing incorrect information. It really is not hard to grasp.

I continued this argument with Steve here, "Well obviously your records are wrong. As I said before, this is NOT the Relaxation Inn."

I felt this should be easy to understand. I know I was not very deep into an argument, but I was speaking very clearly. Even with his apparent need to argue I thought if I just repeated the facts to him a couple of times that I would still manage to end this phone call quickly, but just like Poland in September of 1939 I really was not so lucky.

I heard Steve angrily take a breath. Either this guy was having that bad of a day or he was just that much of a loser. My money is on the latter of the two.

After completing his sullen inhale, my new friend or maybe nemesis Steve once again had to continue our flourishing argument. Sternly he said, "Sir! Look! I really need you to confirm for me that this is indeed the Relaxation Inn."

There was a part of me that just wanted to tell this guy to fuck off and hang up the phone, but there existed a bigger part of me wanted to keep arguing because I really had nothing better to do and was in dire need of entertainment.

I continued our little feud, "Look dude, this is not the Relaxation Inn. I know where I work, and it is not the Relaxation Inn."

I hear a bit of panting on the other end of the line like he was trying to contain himself. He was almost hyperventilating.

After a moment Steve begins again by saying, "Sir, just confirm for me that this is the Relaxation Inn."

It was very apparent that he was really trying not to yell and hold back his anger and frustration instead.

I gave him the response he did not want which was total honesty. So as calmly as I could be I returned fire and said, "Look, I know where I work. I know where I am standing right now. I am looking at the damn sign. This is not the Relaxation Inn. You have the wrong number."

I could not believe what a jackass this guy was. I wanted so badly to show him in person where exactly he was calling. The other part of me wanted to geotag his face to a Pokémon Go game and force him to be swarmed at his office by sugar-infused kids with smartphones.

I could just see myself with some sort of teleportation device that allows me to show up at his work and find him. I could see myself finding the guy in the Travelcon call center. I imagine he would have a giant head with big bug eyes and long gangly arms wearing his jorts and driving gloves because he is just weird like that.

I imagined myself just walking up to him, grabbing him by his enormous head, and dragging him back to the teleportation device that takes us back to the hotel I worked at just, so he could see with his bugged-out eyes that I do not work at the Relaxation Inn.

Our conversation continued and remained redundant. I heard the tapping of a pen on his end and another sigh he let out. Good old Steve was getting even more frustrated.

Steve said, "Just confirm for me already that this is the Relaxation Inn. My records are showing that this is the number to the Relaxation Inn! I NEED you to CONFIRM for me that this is the Relaxation Inn!"

I put my head in my hand. I could not believe how dense this asshole was. This whole ordeal was as amusing as it was annoying. I had to state my piece one more time.

So, I opened my mouth and said to my new BFF Steve, "Dude, I told you. This is not the Relaxation Inn. I know where I work. I know what it says on my paychecks. I am fully aware of where I am standing right now, and I am still looking at the damn sign. So once again this is not the Relaxation Inn. I cannot confirm that for you because it is incorrect."

The tension built even further. It got so high that the tension was almost tangible. I could hear Steve start to hyperventilate again, rising a surfboard of his own tension deep into the Relaxation Inn mountain, crashing, setting himself on fire, then licking the flames out with his slobbering, over insistent tongue. I thought he was going to cry for a moment.

Just then Steve's bottled up anger finally blew a fuse and he could no longer hold it back. Suddenly, he began to yell at me, "YOU'RE A LIAR! YOU'RE A LIAR! YOU'RE A LIAR! STOP LYING TO ME!" Followed up with heavy breathing as Steve tried to catch his breath.

Of course, his reaction to all this and being accused of lying about where I work warranted an equally ridiculous response.

I yelled back, "Y'all don't know me! Don't know what I been through! I killed a man for less!"

There followed a long awkward pause. I covered the mouthpiece of the phone, so I could laugh during the pause. I kept thinking to myself, "Don't break this fucking silence. Don't break this fucking silence." This sentence would become my internal mantra for what was only a couple of minutes but felt like hours.

Finally, Steve broke the silence and said, "Thank you for your time." And then just quickly hung up. I saw this as a victory for me.

I laughed about what I had just experienced for a long time. That had to have been the strangest business to business phone call I had ever experienced.

About two more hours or so had passed since I went through this verbal exchange. When suddenly, the phone rang. I answered like I always do with my brand standard opening speech.

I was greeted on the other end by a woman's voice that said to me, "Good evening sir. My name is Margaret from Travelocon. I am doing a routine call around. I was wondering if you could confirm that I did in fact dial the correct number to reach the Relaxation Inn?"

I paused for moment to hold back laughter. Once I knew I could contain myself I responded to her inquiry by saying, "Actually no this is not the Relaxation Inn." And then proceeded to say where I was working.

Margaret kind of chuckled and said back to me, "Oh okay. My apologies. I will investigate this further. You have a great night." And then hung up the phone.

CALLING INTO WORK DEAD

We all will die at some point. For some, it's a prom night car crash. For others, it's in their beds at 90. And for yet others, it's a year's long process of social abandonment, mid-life crisis purchases, and failed social media hashtags with their kids, ending with a bottle of brandy and a smile into oblivion. It is not a matter of if but when. This is a guarantee for all of us.

In the hotel world it is a guarantee that sooner or later someone will die on property. From peacefully in their sleep of natural causes all the way up to the most violent way possible and anywhere in between. At some point something will happen, and someone will die at least once in a hotel's lifetime. This is not a question of if it will happen but when it will happen. The question is, will you be working when it does?

As I had done for some time, I was working the evening shift. The day was not anything too special. It had not been overly good or bad.

I do not know why much of the absurdity I experienced was at the tail end of my shift, but it was.

So, there I was, standing at the desk. I had a moment of boredom I thought to myself that I wish I could be wearing a red shirt instead, so I could pretend to be the Kool-Aid man.

A man came by the desk. This man had a thick accent, so it was a bit hard to follow him at times. I still listened closely and did my best.

For the purposes of this story I will call this man Dorian. He and his friend Richard had been brought to town by the company they work for. Both men were working an overnight shift as well.

So, Dorian comes by the desk. It was a colder night than he was used to, so he had a heavy coat on. Was in a bit of a hurry. He seemed a bit upset about something and mumbled something about needing to get in his room. I just figured he needed a key.

I said to Dorian, "Hey no worries. I can just make you a new key to your room." As I walked over to our key machine.

Dorian proceeded to stop me. I had misunderstood what he was saying.

He said, "Oh no no no. I have a key. My friend… He is staying with me. He is up in our room and we must go to work. But the latch on the door is locked, and we need to go to work. I think he's asleep but I'm not sure. He won't respond to me."

I threw out the idea that we should just call up to the room and wake Richard up. To which Dorian agreed that this would be a good idea.

I begin to call up to the room and get no answer. I keep trying time and time again and still get no answer. I kept trying and trying and time and time again he did not answer.

Dorian said, "Why don't you keep calling his room phone and I will call his cell phone. That way there is more noise."

"Good idea." I said. "That way there is more noise and I'm sure that will wake him up."

We begin to try that plan. We are trying, and we are trying, and we are trying. There is still no response from him up in their room.

Somewhere in the middle of calling Richard, the night auditor, Blake, showed up to work. He was a bit early and I could not have been happier to see him. I was beginning to become very concerned.

I look at Dorian and he is holding back tears and beginning to sweat. He looks at both of us and said, "Right when we agreed to take this job I promised his family I would look out for him and keep him safe. I promised."

Then Dorian began to tear up. His breathing got heavy as he was wiping his eyes.

I quickly filled Blake in on what was going on. He understood this very well could be an emergency that he was opening his night with.

I said to Blake, "I have a new plan. I need you to stay here and keep calling that room phone over and over and over."

I then turned to Dorian, "You and I are going to go up there and try to get a response out of him."

They both nodded in agreement. I grabbed the master set of keys we kept at the desk and walked around.

The short walk to the elevator Dorian and I took might as well have been ten miles. I kept replaying in my head something that Dave, my general manager, told me, that we haven't had a death in the hotel yet, but it is sadly something we all must accept is going to happen sooner or later.

It's an inevitable progression, unavoidable. Like watching Madonna at 60-something still dress like a 20-year-old-like-a-virgin: sad and inevitable. I braced myself as the elevator continued its snail crawl up to the celestial floors.

The ride up the elevator we were both totally silent. The doors opened, and we stepped off. I was hoping and praying that the phone upstairs was broken, and he slept through his alarm.

I popped the door open as far as I could with the security latch in place. The phone was ringing off the hook with no response. To make matters worse I noticed through the little bit that the door was open that all the lights were on including the bathroom lights. This was a huge red flag.

I began banging on the door, "Sir! Sir can you hear me?!" I continued to bang on the door and yell with total disregard of anyone that might be sleeping.

Dorian even started calling Richard's cell phone and yelling his name into the door alongside me. All this noise and commotion and no response.

"Richard! Richard!" Dorian continued.

I was picturing in my head that we would get the door open and find this guy in the bathroom either having hung himself or overdosed on the floor with a needle still in his arm and foaming at the mouth.

This was an absolute emergency at this point. All that noise and no response. I told Dorian that I am going to go call 911 but to please keep trying him. He said he would, but he would also have to call their employer while he is at it.

I text Blake, "Call 911 now!" and then I start to run down the stairs as I get our general manager on the phone.

I said, "Dave! A guy may have died in a room and the security latch is on the door!"

Dave quickly said, "I'm on my way." And hung up the phone.

By the time I made it down to the desk Blake had just read my text and was picking up the phone to call 911. I explained we don't know if he is alive or what and the security latch is on the door still. Which he then explained to the dispatch operator.

Right after Blake hung up the phone with dispatch Dave calls my phone. He said to just break the security latch because the police will just do it anyway.

I told Blake what Dave had said. He volunteered to go up and do it. Dorian just wanted to sit in the lobby a moment.

Blake walked away towards the elevator. I looked over at Dorian and he is just crying his eyes out and breathing heavy from all the anxiety and anticipation.

He just repeated over and over, "I promised his family I would take care of him! That I would look out for him! I promised nothing bad would happen to him!"

He then said something in his native language that I of course didn't understand.

Blake comes back downstairs alone. He was walking somewhat robotically, and his eyes were wide. My night was becoming ever grimmer.

Blake said, "Okay I got the door open."

Excitingly, Dorian asked, "Is he alive?!"

Blake just responded, "Oh uh, I actually don't know. I just got the door all the way open. I didn't actually go inside…"

All I could picture in my head was Blake opening the door with the master key then kicking the door, so the security latch breaks followed by standing back with a proud look on his face and saying, "Well my work here is done."

Dorian asked him, "Will you go up with me?"

Blake said, "Absolutely." And away they went.

As they started to walk down the hall towards the elevator Blake turns his head back at me and looks at me with his eyes wide and mouths the words "help me."

A moment later I see a police officer probably in his early 30's rushing through the door towards the elevator. He was completely zoned in on getting upstairs.

A moment after the officer had hurried upstairs, a second officer who was middle aged and rather overweight walks in with a civilian ride-along accompanying him. He looked like a real life Chief Wiggum.

The Chief Wiggum officer stopped to ask where the elevator was. I suppose the sign directly across the lobby from him stating where the elevator was located was not obvious. So, I pointed him in the right direction.

A moment after the second officer went upstairs, Dave showed up at the hotel. All of this just happened one after the other like a domino effect. Dave just stayed down at the desk with me instead of going upstairs.

Everyone that had gone upstairs to assess the situation was still there. I looked outside and saw an ambulance and a fire truck. I was certain that I was about to see a man in a body bag being wheeled away.

Dave turned to me and said, "Well I guess we will see what happens now."

I see the police walk out without saying a word to me. I wasn't sure what that meant but everything kept adding up to the worst-case scenario. Shit had really hit the fan that night, flinging its muck of uncertainty on my desk, the walls, everywhere. The stench of inevitable news soaked the walls.

I then see Blake come back down alone and silent. Again, this is all adding up to what we are all expecting is going on here.

I asked, "So, is the dude dead?"

Blake said to me, "No. No he's not actually. We went in there and saw him lying in the bed and we shook him and said his name and he woke right up. Right then the police walked through the door. I guess he that dude was having trouble sleeping so he took something awesome and slept through ALL of that."

"Holy shit!" I said.

Dave chimes in, "Well at least no one died I guess."

Blake then continued on, "Yeah the fat cop guy wasn't too happy. He was going off about how this sounds like a false report or some bullshit. I told him that no we legitimately thought a dude was dead or well on his way there and he should just be thankful that no one did die."

Adding his two cents Dave said, "Well you guys did the right thing for calling and since there was no issue after all he can just leave. He doesn't need to be harassing my staff."

Dave took off back home not long after. I stuck around a bit to fill out my incident report since the police arrived.

Dorian came by the desk again. He was looking a bit shook up still but still more relieved than not.

I asked, "Hey man, you doing okay?"

He said, "Yeah I will be okay. I am just glad he is alive."

"I think we all are." I said, "You sure you guys are going to be alright?"

Dorian said, "Yes, thank you. I am just so thankful he is alive, and nothing happened to him. Our employers gave us the night off still and said not to worry about coming in."

"That was nice of them. I guess who would want to come in after that much less be able to actually function at work correctly?" I said back.

Dorian shook his head in agreement and said to me, "Well it is better to be given the night off from work than calling into work dead."

In that moment I did consider what it would be like to call into work one day that I just don't feel like going and say I'm calling in dead. I doubt it would be received as well as I would like.

He walked over to me and shook mine and Blake's hands and gave us both hugs and thanked us repeatedly before going back upstairs.

I went home after that. I had to repeat this story many times over the next few days following that experience. Naturally so it is now ending up here being told to you.

FAT GUY EXPOSE'

Some things just hit us by surprise, and they are not always positive surprises: an unwanted pregnancy, a sudden death in the family, a new Daft Punk album (they should have stopped in 2002).

I went my entire shift without any sort of abnormality or issue I had to deal with. Not even a noise complaint.

Call me pessimistic, but I could not help but feel as though this was all too good to be true. I really did want to believe this day would be bullshit free, but I also knew I just wasn't that lucky.

I was checking my shirt for stains or missing buttons or anything wrong with my work clothes. I was sure something even that small had to happen. It was like hotel karma: one flawless shift means you get a flat tire going home or find Rachel Maddow as your new roommate.

Eventually I just accepted that this was a seemingly good day. It was quiet, no complaints, no one being rude or obnoxious. I was about to have that one in a million perfect work days.

At one point in the evening one of our semi-regular guests came to check in.

Her name was Delores. She was some sort of regional manager of a chain of salons. She was always friendly, enjoyed her stays, and happily returned.

At one-point other employees of her company seemed to come to town instead of her. Sometimes we would see her still but after a while it was mostly one of her coworkers. They were all very nice and personable, so we happily went out of our way to go above and beyond for them.

A brief caveat here… If you are nice and friendly with the staff at a hotel they will take notice and they will be more likely to do a lot of nice things for you even without you asking.

Delores came to town that night and checked in. Everything was straight forward. Nothing abnormal.

I am going to fast forward here. A perfect work day where no sorts of fuckery take place is seriously like winning the lottery.

I got very close. I mean I got VERY close. All I needed was the last "Powerball" multiplier for the jackpot.

That day I was working the 3pm-11pm shift. I looked at the time and it was 10:58pm. I thought to myself, "This is awesome! I am almost out of here and no one has fucked up my day for me!" The night auditor had just walked in. Then the phone rang... It was Delores' room calling...

Delores said, "Ummm... So... There is some guy outside my window..."

"That's creepy. I will go tell him he needs to leave before I call the police." I said.

But of course, things can never be that simple. She said, "Well you may just want to call them anyway. He is kind of... exposing himself to me..."

There was a small gap between the curtains in her room. And through this small gap that was left open was this man peering in and exposing his genitals. Of course, the one time she ever stays on the ground floor this happens.

"Oh my God!" I said. "Just stay in your room. I'm going to call the police."

"Well I'm going to get his attention and go outside and try to talk to him. I want to know what his problem is." Delores said.

I was not expecting this response. So, I said, "I really do not suggest that, but I can't stop you."

I get off the phone and start to make my way out from behind the desk. Matt asked, "Where are you going off to?"

"I'm going to go kick his ass!" I replied.

I ran towards the backdoor and outside as fast as I could. I planned on calling the police after this man's ass kicking. I did not see anyone right away. I looked to the right down the parking lot and then the left. I saw Delores beginning to walk around the left side of the building towards the front. So as quick as I could I ran back in the backdoor and through the lobby out the front doors.

Delores and I see each other, and we walk towards each other.

I asked, "What happened?"

To which she said, "Well once he noticed that I noticed him he got a little freaked out and kind of started to waddle off towards his car, so I ran outside. I was hoping to get him to come inside with me and then I was going to beat his ass with a heel and make him wait until the police arrived."

"So, I take it you didn't catch him?" I said.

Delores took a quick sigh and said, "No, sadly for a fat guy he is really fast. He sort-of ran off while trying to pull up his pants and got into a red car and drove off as soon as I got out here."

Delores looks down the street a bit. "See! That's the car!" She said.

I didn't see it where I was standing. I was right in a blind spot with some trees and other buildings.

I asked her, "So what exactly happened? I know you gave me part of the story, but I really just got to know."

Delores began to go back over this recent happening. She was just sitting there on the bed watching some TV and saw some movement outside the window as she had stated. She got up a little bit and just saw this large guy wearing a red hat, grey shirt, and khaki shorts (which were around his knees at the time). He saw her movement and got freaked out and drove off.

I asked, "Did you get a good look at him?"

Delores said, "Well yeah... I kind of saw all of him."

Her plan with talking to him was to act somewhat interested and get him to come inside and beat his ass with a heel until the police arrived.

I called the police for her. I just told them that a man was outside a guest's room exposing himself. I don't know if it was more disturbing that this was going on or that the 911 operator did not seem at all surprised. Matt, my night auditor, had a look of shock, confusion, and disgust.

The police show up a few minutes or so later. Delores had been just waiting in the lobby with me.

Two police officers walk into the lobby. They all greet each other and one of the officers said to her, "Well I am sorry if this was your first exposure to our town here. Pardon the pun."

After a bit of laughter died down they asked if she could describe him. She brought her hand up to about right under her nose and said, "He was about this tall. And he was wearing a red hat, grey shirt, and khaki shorts which he had pulled down, so his genitals were exposed. Oh, and he was probably a good 300 pounds. He was white... Probably around 50 years old." She pointed over to me, "I told him all of this too."

One of the officers had this grossed out look on his face and said, "So we are looking for a short, morbidly obese middle-aged guy?"

The first officer said, 'Let's go over here and talk for a bit." Signaling over to the breakfast bar area. They walked over and sat down to fill out the police report.

I proceeded to the back office to fill out an incident report.

I just stared at the sheet for a while. Not seeing anything on there about a man exposing his genitals to a guest. Eventually I just gave up and wrote down in the blank space what happened.

How crazy is this though? What are the chances that some creep like this is driving around and sees shades on the bottom floor of a hotel room partly open and an unexpected person hanging out minding their own business and he just thinks "Jackpot!"

Amazingly enough she continued to come back. She was at least understanding enough that she knew it wasn't the hotel's fault. Of course, we never again put her on the first floor. Oh, and a perfect shift still alludes me to this day, as I'm sure the following stories will elucidate...

THE FRUMPTRIST

A lot of people in the world claim to have bigfoot sightings. If you were to plug the topic into Google, you would get countless pages on the subject. They are about as common as fake rumors that Morgan Freeman died again this year* (*Note, if Morgan Freeman is dead at the time of this writing, I am sorry).

Along with all the various claims of people seeing Bigfoot, you also have at least as many people debunking the subject.

This brings me to this story. It is about a truly unforgettable character.

There was this person who I would see once a year every year. I cannot stand this person. This person is a woman. At least I can only assume.

She looks like if the Stay Puffed Marshmallow guy from Ghostbusters managed to squeeze into some sort of Pippi Longstocking bodysuit costume thing, and then put on the frumpiest clothes imaginable. Clothing so frumpy they had to be custom made. I call her The Frumptrist.

She was just all-around frumpy person, and I hated her. Not because of her frumpiness but because she was just such a bitchy whiny horrible person. The frump wasn't winning her any prizes though. It did add a bit to my antipathy.

She would always wear the same red, yellow, and green long sleeve plaid button up shirt. Her shirt was like if Christmas fell down the ugly tree, became paralyzed, was put in a wheelchair and was called a shirt. It had giant frills in the shoulders accompanied by an oddly large collar. She kept her shirt tucked into her 80's mom jeans with bell bottoms that she hiked up well past her waist. To complete the ensemble, she had this rainbow colored, off brand, cowboy boots with tassels hanging from them.

It is hard to say whether someone chose to dress this frumpy or she as a person is just so frumpy that her clothing just magically adapted to the amount of frump.

The Frumptrist also had a friend with her. This friend was a nondescript woman who always wore the same denim dress and never said a single word ever. She was constantly right by the Frumptrist. It is my assumption that this woman was the Frumptrist's horcrux.

I will never forget the first time the Frumptrist came to check in.

I see the Frumptrist and her horcrux beginning to march in the front doors. I really was having trouble figuring out if what I was seeing was real or imaginary. Or if it was real how could this person not be doing this as a joke? I by no means am any sort of fashion icon. I barely can dress myself half the time, but I don't exactly go out of my way to dress like I walked off the set of a movie taking place in some dystopian future. Or maybe perhaps this wardrobe of hers is just another appendage and/or otherwise an extension of her body.

I decided to put all of this out of my mind for a moment. They were approaching, and I was going to have to check them in.

I see them and look at each other. The Frumptrist then quietly said something the two then left. I thought for a moment that my brain had started melting.

Momentarily following, the phone rang. As my job dictates, I answered and began to help the person on the other line.

Well right in the middle of it, the Frumptrist suddenly appeared before me out of frumpy air. Standing a bit behind her nearby one of the lobby chairs was her horcrux friend.

I was obviously right in the middle of helping this person on the phone. This did not stop her from repeatedly slapping the desk and saying, "Uhhh! Hello?! I would like to CHECK IN!"

Remaining calm among her rude behavior I covered the mouthpiece of the phone to say to her, "I will be right with you."

The Frumptrist just rolled her eyes and let out a moan in annoyance. She then said to me, "I would like to get some help here! Hello?!"

Trying to ignore her rudeness and wrap up this conversation I just repeated myself, "I will be right with you." As I covered the mouthpiece of the phone.

She grew more impatient. I was waiting for her shoulder ruffles to shoot out venomous spikes. Or her large, cartoon like, teeth to turn into fangs. Basically, for her to turn into Joy Behar.

The Frumptrist threw her arms in the air, began to move around a bit as she said, "Tick tock! This is getting ridiculous!"

Her foot started to tap. The ceiling lights reflected off the cheap rhinestones she had bedazzled her boots with.

I was already in no rush to get off the phone. If she was going to be this rude she could wait is what I figured.

I was just about done with this phone conversation when this person whom I believe to be a woman said, "Oh my God! This is fucking ridiculous! What does it take to get real customer service these days?"

It is truly amazing how rude and entitled people get. This instance was a new one for me though.

Being as snarky as I am, I decided not to end the call just yet. If she was going to be a shitty person then she can wait even longer.

I asked the gentleman on the other line, "So what is bringing you guys to town?"

He said, "Oh just visiting some family in the area."

His response was generic and almost expected, but this made it easier for me to carry on a conversation with him.

The Frumptrist scoffed at me and said, "Uh... Hello?!"

So, I turned my back to her and continued to have this conversation with this gentleman on the phone.

Eventually I got off the phone with the Frumptrist standing at the desk glaring at me. She probably wanted to kill me.

She did not say a word to me during check in. Her friend who may or may not be the Frumptrist's horcrux stood there perfectly still the whole time. I swear she did not blink even once either. Evidently, Steven Spielberg found his next casting model for the Frankenstein remake.

I think the Frumptrist's given name was like Mildred or some name that should have died in the 1920s. It was some frumpy name you give your frumpy child because you hate them, and you know they are going to grow up to be just... just awful.

Throughout the week I would be minding my own business only to look and see the alleged horcrux standing a short way across from me in her denim dress just staring with her lifeless gaze. I was not sure if she was staring at me or not. Or anything at all.

Then, out of frumpy air, comes the Frumptrist entering stage left each time.

She would walk into my line of sight and pause, turn her head towards me, glare, and then finish it off with a creepy circus clown smile. At first it was funny but then after a while it was just creepy, and I thought I was going to be murdered.

I guess if an epic battle were to take place I would spring towards the woman in the denim vest. After all she contains the Frumptrist's powers and her secret to immortality. There really was no other explanation for her and I will not hear otherwise.

They made their way out the door to go to this convention. Their absence, albeit brief, brought me much joy.

One day I had to inquire if one of my coworkers had seen this woman who is allegedly human and/or was developed by Steve Jobs before he died as a sick joke to share with underperforming coworkers. He looked at me extremely confused. I asked a couple more coworkers and they did not know who I was speaking of either.

I was starting to think I should start some sort of website where others could post their Frumptrist sightings much like one would for bigfoot or UFO's.

The remainder of the week was getting random glimpses of these two walking by and glaring at me and from time to time the Frumptrist would come by the desk to say to me, "Well it looks like someone wore their big boy pants today."

I would usually follow this statement up with a look of utter confusion while saying, "Um… What?"

The Frumptrist would manage to somehow hike up her pants a bit further after this and say, "Well let that be a lesson to ya!"

I did not then, and I still do not understand this. Everything about this was confusing. Nothing at all made sense. What she said did not make sense. Her intonation made no sense. What in the hell does that mean?

Fake news was Frumpist before it was Trumpist.

Every year they would come back, and it would be like some sort of Groundhog Day repeat of when I first encountered them.

Year after year I would have to check them in and receive the same obnoxious behavior from them. This would always be followed up with their death glares and the weird comments.

I felt like I was doomed to dealing with the Frumptrist and the other one in all their frumpy glory (or some sort of antithesis thereof) and being as I seemed to be the only one who knew who these two were, I was doomed to go through this alone.

If there is a hell, I had truly found it.

UNACCEPTABLE

I was working the evening shift when this all transpired. It was shortly after Labor Day when the summer is now officially over, and school sports haven't really started yet so it would normally be dead at the hotel, but on that day, we had a full house. In fact, every hotel in town had a full house. No rhyme or reason for it. No events going on in town. No groups or sports or anything really happening. Everywhere in town was just sold out.

Not only was it a sold-out night but our guests that night were just so damn needy. We were dealing with a full house of the neediest and entitled asshole guests ever. It's as if Kim and Kanye had another child, named it after another compass direction, then decided to stay at my hotel with all their friends. So, we were all just running around like chickens with our heads cut off all night trying to appease these people.

For example, one guest checked into a single king room. Nothing over the top. Just a regular standard room that happens to have one king sized bed in it. Well these snobby entitled assholes get up to their room and every damn thing in it is wrong to them. They just assumed by king bed that we meant California King. They assumed that this room, while not being a suite, would have a whirlpool tub.

They asked for an extra blanket. I grabbed one and brought it up to their room. They then called the desk to complain that it was not a "king sized blanket" even though yes it was. It even says so on the damn tag. Oh, and let's not forget that they expected a 65-inch television and their night was now ruined over the lack thereof.

That is just some quick examples of what I was dealing with that night. For hours I dealt with a cacophony of people such as that.

The night continued to progress and if it was not guests being a pain in my ass it was the constant barrage of phone calls and people walking in off the streets to see if we had any rooms available. All these people became upset with me when I had to be the bearer of bad news that we did not have any rooms open and no one in town does. The entire city was a virgin before her wedding night. Closed.

It was not until the last hour of my shift that everything finally died down. It was a ghost town for that last hour. I really did not care that it was only an hour of peace and quiet. After all that ANY amount of peace and quiet was paradise.

Roughly two minutes before the end of my shift the night auditor (we will call him Dave) showed up to work. He comes in and gets clocked in as one does.

Dave comes up to the desk and we count down the register together as is the custom. Then I gave him the rundown on the shit show that was that day.

Then it happened. That scrawny little bald head fuck walked through those doors.

This guy was a bit on the shorter end. He was skinny, wore glasses, and balding. He was not completely bald yet. What little hair he had left was a dark brown. His hair was clinging to his scalp like a Baby Boomer still clings to have relevance. He had that whole horseshoe thing going on with his hair and had that like little tuft of hair on the top nearing his forehead like his head has a soul patch because the top of his head still lives in 1999.

So there Dave and I are just switching out shifts and this guy walks in. He walks up but doesn't turn towards us to face us. He remains with his side turned towards us. He paused and didn't turn his head towards us either.

After a couple of seconds, he opens his mouth and almost robotically says, "The hotel next door to you has said you are sold out. Can you confirm?"

First, this guy was not even facing us. I know I tend to be weird and awkward as fuck but at least I understand that when you are speaking with someone you generally want to face them. Obviously, like with anything, there are exceptions, but this is not one of them.

I did give him the benefit of the doubt though because just my luck I am going to blow up on him and it is going to turn out he has a hearing or vision problem.

After a quick pause Dave and I looked at each other and I said to this man, "Yeah man, we are sold out completely. The whole town is right now."

This man just stood there completely still. He did not even blink. Dave and I had to look at each other to make sure we were each seeing this. He stood there for close to 20 seconds and finally said, "Unacceptable" in the most deadpan voice ever. Which is thus why I have dubbed him with the name "Unacceptable Guy."

I was a bit lost for words at first. Dave just jumped in and told him, "Sorry man, we are sold out. Wish I could do more for ya."

Unacceptable Guy turned towards us at this point and took a step closer to the desk. His eyes were wide. He had this look on his face like he ate something rather sour but also needed to express a bit of anger and hostility.

This conversation was not over for him yet. In his deadpan robot voice, he inquired, "Why? What is going on that nowhere in town would have an open room available?"

Still having to take a moment before speaking I finally opened my mouth to say to him, "Sorry, there is really no reason for it. Just kind of a freak thing tonight. Everywhere is just sold out. No rhyme or reason."

He then puts his elbows on the desk, interlaces his fingers together while pushing his two index fingers together and places them right under his bottom lip as if he was deep in thought. Then he took a breath and uttered the word, "Unacceptable." He probably hisses that word when he orgasms, wins the lottery or takes a shit. It seems his mantra.

I was barely into this conversation with him and my patience was growing thin. Maybe it was from the day I had. Maybe it was from the fact that I am not sure if this jackass is an alien or a robot or some sort of alien cyborg but not the cool kind. Maybe it was both things, but I was already getting sick and tired of him standing in my lobby.

I quickly found a middle ground to both show my irritation but also still find a way to be at least nice enough that no one above me can get mad. Meanwhile Dave was looking online to make sure there were indeed no rooms left in town.

I said in a sterner tone of voice, "Look, we have no rooms. No one in town has any rooms either. There is nothing going on. Just a freak thing. Good luck to you."

He decides to say his favorite word again like a good little cyborg, "Unacceptable." He continued, "There must be some sort of reason or function going on in town that everywhere is sold out. And you will tell me IMMEDIATELY!" As he puffed out his frail bony chest and made a face like Derek Zoolander with a hint of anger.

I knew he was trying to come off as intimidating. But this was just stupid. He was just stupid.

I just said to him, "Look dude. There is nothing going on in town."

He grew a little more impatient and said his favorite word, "Unacceptable!"

I quickly responded, "You're unacceptable."

Dave quickly tried to be somewhat diplomatic and maintain good customer service by saying, "Well hold on. I'll call the hotel over by the hospital. People usually forget about that one."

Sure, enough they did not have any rooms either. Unacceptable guy at this point threw his arms in the air and pumped his fists and yelled, "Unacceptable!" Dave's eyes just got huge. He whispered to me asking him if he should call the police. I told him to just hold on a second. I was sure this weaselly little wide-eyed asshole in our lobby was ultimately harmless.

I think Dave knew that I was about to get even more snarky with this guy and politely reiterated that we were indeed sold out and could not further help him.

This guy stood there in silence and glared. One more time he had to say to us, "Unacceptable."

I was about ready to punch him in the face. After the long day I had I was not in any mood to be dealing with his bullshit.

Apparently, it was not game over just yet. He began to rant about his journey and his issues finding a hotel room to stay in for the night. He began to lament, "I've actually been driving across the country. I'm from Canada. I was going to stop in the city that was about an hour south of here. There were plenty of hotels, but I would drive up to them and couldn't find the entrance. They were horribly engineered."

My question of course for him was, "So you're telling me that you drove up to these hotels and since you did not, at first glance, see a front door so you thought it wasn't worth trying to drive around until you found the fucking door?"

Unacceptable Guy gave me a dirty look and said, "Unacceptable."

For some reason Dave went from feeling as though he may need to call the police to wanting to engage this guy in conversation by asking, "So what brings you down here from Canada?"

I turned to Dave and gave him the most annoyed "I will fucking kill you" look I could give him.

Unacceptable Guy, now being further enabled, told us his little tale. "Well I've been driving across the United States, for this trip anyway, for almost two weeks now. My plan is to head back to Canada soon but only briefly. I need to hide from the government before they draft me" he said.

As if I needed any more proof that this dude was off his rocker. I just had to ask, "Since when does Canada have a draft?"

Of course, he had to give me one more "Unacceptable." He continued, "Well obviously you wouldn't know because you aren't in the know. However, since I am in a good mood I will educate you. There has always been a draft in both the United States and Canada. It has just been secret. They can take you from your home and put you in the army... Now if you'll excuse me I should be going before the CIA catches me."

His ludicrous and nonsensical rant gave me an opening that I could not pass up. I cheerfully said to him with a smile on my face, "Well I'm afraid it's a little too late for that now. You see, I am a CIA operative. In fact, so is Dave here!"

The look of horror on his face was wonderfully over exaggerated and almost like that of an anime character. He ran out of the lobby as fast as he could. That made up for the crappy night I had just endured.

MARY THE METH-HEAD HOOKER

"I like cocaine and prostitutes because they are a fun thing to do."
-Former US Representative Robert Wexler
interviewed on The Colbert Report

Mary the meth-head!
Liked to stay at our hotel!
She was made of blow and the Johns all know
That 40 bucks gets her all day!

Yes, that is to the tune of Frosty the Snowman.

Meth... It's a hell of a drug. I have never tried it but seeing other people on it makes me curious just how quickly I could clean my bathroom, or throw out other meth heads from my hotel... Don't worry, it's never going to happen: why inject poison into your veins when the ambient toxicity of your average guest gives you enough of a rush? Anyways, here is a story about how a hooker named Mary fucked up.

This meth loving hooker named Mary decided to check in for a night at my hotel and thus begin her shenanigans.

Imagine a perfect-looking Barbie doll. Then throw it out and imagine Mary: She was pale with ratty unkempt blond hair. Her persistent meth use stretched too little skin over too thin and long a frame.

She wore what must have been several pounds of makeup to not only draw in more clients but to appear as though she is still a functioning human being. Although this was a failure for her. From a mile away, you could see she was wearing copious amounts of red-neck war paint being used as make-up. I was wondering if she was going to start offering me a balloon to lower me into a sewer. Like straight out of a Stephen King story.

Before she arrived, a man showed up to get the room that she would be ultimately staying in. This man's name was Roy. Logic would dictate that he was her pimp. Maybe a druggy boyfriend but I like to add some excitement to my life. He just pulls up, walks in, books the room under his name with his card and had us list her as the accompanying guest.

When he arrived, there was a black truck that pulled up and a white car. The car drove off with Roy and the black truck stayed. We did not see Roy again after this.

So, she comes in a bit later and due to her obvious drug use, sores, makeup, and attire that was like something out of a bad vice detective cop drama; it was obvious to me why she was there. Some of the other staff was not entirely convinced though.

So that first evening she had a string of male visitors coming in and out. To be honest no one would have noticed had she been smart about this. This is a hotel we are talking about. People come and go at all hours. If they all just minded their own business, it would not have been overtly obvious who was there to exchange sexual favors with her for meth money.

She obviously was not in the least bit intelligent though. She had her clientage come by the front desk and give the room number, the last name it was booked under, and ask for a key to the room.

The next morning, she extended her stay another night. To my knowledge the plan was to tell her we were booked up, so she could not extend. However, somewhere along the way, this got lost in translation with my coworker who was working the desk that morning. So, she was able to extend her stay another night. Imagine a snake eating its own tail. Then forget that and just be a meth-addicted hooker looking to extend your stay at our establishment.

She checks out and not only has the room been smoked in, but used needles nestled themselves in the trash like silver haystacks. Roy, her pimp or druggy boyfriend or whatever he was, was now being charged a nice fee for the smoking, and we had to find a sharps container to dispose the needles. Some of my coworkers argued with me that it could have been used for insulin ("You never know, I've seen all kinds of diabetes technology,") and not for meth or heroin or something.

Later, a new, prepaid, reservation came in for her. This time it was under her name and not this Roy guy's name, so it was not noticed right away. On top of this, she didn't even come to check in. She sent some guy in to check in for her.

So, this guy, who I can only guess was some sort of provider of her illicit substances and activities, came to check in early afternoon. He was taller greying hair. His name was Matt. Which made sense since he kind of looked like a doormat.

Not long after checking in we noticed there was the same black truck parked outside, and of course due to this woman's brain on drugs, we shortly thereafter saw her walking around strung out asking if anyone had shown up looking for her.

I recall this conversation so well. It went like this:

Mary mumbled something incomprehensible and then said to me, "Is there like any guys coming all around here looking for me and stuff?"

I responded, "Oh God I hope not. Hey what room are you in?"

We needed her room number to begin this process of kicking her out. But alas, she wandered off mumbling more incomprehensible noises.

The next morning, we learned of her room number being as she came by the desk to extend and we told her once again that we were sold out and could not extend her reservation.

Sure enough, more needles were found, like ship masts looming out of a sea of tacky red carpet and this time she had dyed her hair and ruined some of the towels.

Some time had passed. We were still on the lookout for her return. This seemed inevitable to all of us.

As I am sure you have guessed just following the flow of this story, she did indeed make a triumphant return.

Once again, this wannabe pimp Roy makes the reservation for her. This time he made the reservation online and then emailed in a credit card authorization form, so she could check in with his card.

For whatever reason, our morning shift person that day, still let her check in.

Maybe the morning person just forgot entirely who she was or maybe they deep down decided we needed more guest drama involving meth and hookers… Either way they let this lady come back.

I must give credit where credit is due. Julie was still a very nice lady. She was the type of person who would have shared needles with you had you asked. So altruistic really.

I really wanted her gone as soon as possible. We deal with enough freaks and weirdos as it is at work. I really did not want a bunch of people who look like they are here for the Steve Buscemi look-alike contest showing up and trying to dig the bugs out of their skin. That whole situation seems like it could be very avoidable.

Apparently, I am just an asshole for wanting to kick her out immediately. Sure, I mean I suggested that we stage a police raid and watch her run out screaming. I figured if we just banged on her door and told her to get out there would be a scene anyway. At least with my idea it would be funny.

Let us just imagine for a moment this woman hanging out in her hotel room and by a series of simple gestures of the staff claiming to be police out in the halls and playing a siren noise on someone's phone, we convince her, in all her paranoid tweaker glory, that the police are after her.

We could even take it a step further and have her believe that the police also want to steal her stash. Her reaction would have been amazing. Although it may have ended in several broken windows.

It was made loud and clear that she had to check out and if she wanted to extend that we would tell her we were sold out.

For that evening though I still had to deal with her paranoid meth delusions where she thought someone was calling her room or yelling at her through the window even though, not only do they not open, but she was on the 3rd floor.

She had many "visitors" as one would imagine. These guys made it a little too obvious when they would come in and give the specific room number and ask where it is. Then after the scabs and rotting teeth were done flying during their meth filled prostitute sex, these guys who came by to see her would leave out the back entrance.

As luck would have it, right after everyone on staff is verbally told the memo, it is the time she did not try to extend her stay, and once again there were cigarette butts, dirty needles, and a small baggie of methamphetamine found.

Something had to be done once and for all to just end this. Dana, my front desk manager, finally listened to my suggestion of just calling this Roy guy and telling them they're both not allowed back.

He calls Roy to break the news to him. I don't think anyone was expecting how he reacted. I mean sure, he was going to be upset but this was just amazing.

So, Dana calls Roy and says who he is and then goes on to say, "So just so you know, we found dirty needles and methamphetamine in the room and the room had been smoked in. I am calling to inform you that you guys will no longer be able to stay here. Also, since meth was found we have informed the police."

Roy must have been having a bad trip that day. He immediately gets scared and paranoid and in this squeaky high-pitched voice he says, "What?! I'm going to jail?! Oh no!"

Dana continued, "Well I did say we had to alert the police."

Roy again shrieked, "Oh no! I'm going to jail."

Another man's voice in the background said, "What what is going on?!"

Roy said to Dana, "Hold on my brother is here." Then continued to speak with his brother crying, "I'm going to jail! They're gonna arrest me!"

His brother expeditiously responded saying, "What?! Oh no! What is gonna happen to me?!" Oh no!"

Roy carried forward bawling, "Who cares! I'm going to jail!" Anyone within 10 feet of the phone could hear the tears running down his face. No one ever said he was an intelligent pimp. He probably doesn't even have a fur coat and a cup encrusted with diamonds.

Roy's brother asked, "Why is this happening? Why are you going to jail?"

Roy, still sobbing and drenched in his meth contaminated tears, responded, "Because of Julie!"

"What?!" Roy's brother responded.

Roy screamed, "BECAUSE OF MARY!!!"

His brother began to cry, "Oh no!" In a high-pitched squeal.

Dana followed up with, "Well I do need to point out again that there was smoking in the room, so we will also be having to charge you an additional $250."

Roy was still crying and dreading what he thinks is going to happen, "Well who gives a shit? I'm going to jail anyway."

Prostitution and meth is lucrative, so I can't imagine this druggy boyfriend or possible drug peddling pimp would not be able to afford a

$250 smoking charge. I mean one probably could if they weren't like him and shooting his money into his arm.

Roy and his brother continue to cry and have their moment of panic that lead to Roy just hanging up the phone.

A few minutes later after he had composed himself he called us back.

Attempting to hold back tears and most likely still strung out, Roy said, "So do you think if I call the jail they will tell me what is going to happen to me?"

Dana, seeing an opening for something jocular, said, "Well if I were you I would I would certainly call and ask."

Roy said, "Well I guess I better call and see what they will do to me then." And begins crying again.

Within milliseconds I had this mental imagery of this Roy guy taking a hit from his meth pipe and calling the nearest correctional facility to him.

They would answer the phone and his sobbing would begin as he said, "Because of Mary! I'm going to jail because of Mary! What are you going to do to me now?! Are you coming to get me?! IT WAS MARY!!!!! Mary is my whore! She did it but I'm going to jail! COME TAKE ME AWAY!"

He would of course just get hung up on and his meth-head paranoia would convince him that he is being hunted. Roy would then live in a tree in a park somewhere until one day he would steal a kid's bicycle and ride it off a cliff thinking he is in the final scene of "Thelma and Louise."

Meanwhile Mary probably ended up in prison where she would start a musical theater group that would fail miserably.

I am choosing to believe this is what happened and why they never tried to sneak back in.

STRANDED FLIGHT CREW

One afternoon we received a call from a flight crew up at the airport. Their flight had been cancelled and they were told they basically had the freedom to pick where they wanted to stay for the night. So, they decided to call and book a room at my hotel.

While I am not going to give away the name of the airline company they work for; I will say that it is named after a landform that forms from the deposition of sediment carried by a river.

They checked in and the rest of the night went on without incident. They kept to themselves and there was no real problem with anyone.

This may seem anticlimactic but really what happened was not during their stay but after. It has to do with the phone call I received the next morning after their departure.

Bright and early in the morning we took them up to the airport when they scheduled to have us take them. They left and there appeared to be no issue.

About 30 minutes after the shuttle driver had returned from the airport the phone rang. It would be one of the phone calls that would make me hate speaking to anyone on the phone while at work.

I answered the phone as I would always while at work. I was greeted on the other line by a man working for the airport.

The man said to me, "Yes, this is Geraldo. I work up here at the airport."

Geraldo had this very annoyed sound to his voice and was breathing a bit heavy.

"Hi, how can I help you," I said.

Geraldo took a deep breath before speaking. I do not know if his lung capacity was that bad or the sound of my voice just pissed him off that much. Either of these does seem logical.

Geraldo continued, "So uh... You had a flight crew staying there last night... And uh... They were supposed to get a ride to the airport this morning from you guys."

Not being sure if he was just wanting to tell me things or if he was going somewhere with this I asked, "Yes sir, we took them up about 45 minutes ago. Is there something I can help you with?"

Obviously not listening to me Geraldo said, "So… They were like supposed to have checked in 30 minutes ago. I would like to know why exactly you guys have not brought them up here yet. They have a plane to fly today,"

We seriously took them up there about 45 minutes ago at this point. I can only imagine he did not see them come in because he was too busy smearing peanut butter on his face while listening to Billy Joel.

My response to him was, "Well as I said sir we took them up already. In fact, that was about 45 minutes ago now."

I managed to upset him by saying this. Geraldo went on to say, "Well actually sir, you did not bring them up here because they did not check in. So, you need to tell me where they are."

I can only imagine that after they got out of the shuttle van that this flight crew somehow stepped through a portal into Narnia or some shit. At least I hope that is what happened. That would be cool. And I can't imagine any of this crew wouldn't enjoy the excitement.

I had to once again had to tell him the extent of what had happened from the time they got in the van that morning, "Well you see sir, the crew got into the shuttle van. Upon which our driver took them up to the airport. After our driver pulled the van in front of the doors there the crew then got out of the very van that took them up there. Then they walked inside, and the driver came back to the hotel. All of this took place about 45 minutes ago. We have no idea of their whereabouts since then."

Geraldo's quick retort was, "Well you are going to need to tell me where they are right now!"

I decided to just give a short simple answer. I was imagining that his mind had a hard time comprehending too much talking. I said, "Well you might just want to call them and ask them where they are. They sure as hell aren't here."

Geraldo grew angrier with me. He told me, "Sir! I will have your job if you do not tell me exactly where this flight crew is and get them here in a timely manner! So, start talking mister unless you want to be without a job within the hour!"

This is not the first time some sort of outside person was upset about something that was out of my control and then threatened my job out of some sort of hubris thought that they can determine whether I am employed. This would also not be the last time this would happen either.

I just said, "Look man, I already told you we dropped them off. If they are screwing around somewhere that's on them. You don't need to try to flex muscle you don't have by threatening my job. That just wouldn't happen anyway. Why don't you look up someone's cell number and give them a call to chew them out and stop wasting my time."

It was at this point where the floodgates of his wrath opened. He began to yell, "I'M GONNA CALL THE POLICE AND THE DEPARTMENT OF HOMELAND SECURITY AND THE TSA! THEY'RE GOING TO TALK TO YOUR MANAGER AND YOU ARE GOING TO LOSE YOUR JOB! THEN YOU WILL HAVE TO GO TO JAIL! DO YOU WANT THAT?! DO YOU WANNA GO TO JAI..."

Before he could finish the word jail I just hung up the phone. I was not angry or anything. I was laughing super hard and had to hang up because I needed both hands to wipe my tears. The thought of several law enforcement agencies showing up at my work to have my manager fire me and haul me off to jail for a flight crew's irresponsibility created this wonderful scenery in my head.

Later that day Geraldo's boss called the hotel to apologize. Through laughing once again at our verbal exchange I eventually was able to tell his boss that it's all right and that I found it funny.

Maybe I am the stupid one though. Even after this conjuncture I continue to fly in and out of that very airport.

HE SEEMED NORMAL
AT FIRST

$$\text{C}\text{IIII}\text{O}$$

People who we identify as insane, often, appear normal. A prime example of this is serial killers. Go ahead and look up famous serial killers. Most of them seem like every day normal and even nice-looking people.

I should get this out of the way right now that this story does not involve a serial killer. At least not to my knowledge. If that was the case I would be devoting a whole book to that not just a chapter. This story is however, involving a clinically insane person as you probably have guessed.

Our story begins on one of my infamous overnight shifts. Plenty of crazy moments happen at other times but it seems late at night is when all the freaks and weirdos come out. So naturally I would be available to work those shifts.

I remember that day well. I was going to work feeling optimistic. I had not had anything weird or crazy happen for some time. I felt like I was on a winning streak. Way to jinx myself.

I get to work and clock in. The evening person, Beth, had to break some bad news to me.

She said, "So I think I may have just checked in a crazy guy."

I immediately stopped and looked at her with disappointment and confusion before I said, "What do you mean you think you may have checked in a crazy guy?"

"Well he seemed normal at first," Beth said.

My look of disappointment and confusion now became a look of abhorrence peppered with irritation. I knew this was going to become quite the untimely event. The non-verbal communication I could relay was much more expressive than anything verbal.

"Just tell me what happened. I need to know what kind of crazy we are dealing with here," I said.

Beth went on to say, "Well he comes in needing a room. So, I get him one. He seemed totally normal. He isn't weird looking or anything. Maybe a bit dirty like someone who works outside in construction but nothing to be concerned about. He had a driver's license and his credit card worked. It all was fine until he took the keys from my hand and said something about how he is in hiding because 'they' are after him. Now he keeps randomly calling the desk and hanging up."

All I could think to say was, "Well who is after him supposedly?"

"I don't know," She said, "He is obviously off his meds. I am sorry. I guess just call the police and have him removed if he becomes too much of problem."

Beth clocks out and leaves for the night. Leaving me there alone not knowing what was going to happen. Still hopeful that he will just keep to himself.

My mind came up with a couple scenarios of how the events of this night were about to unfold.

First my imagination went somewhere dark. I imagined my night beginning quiet and calm and then suddenly hearing blood curdling screams. Upon investigating this I would find this man in a psychotic episode and this guy is just chopping up bodies with gardening equipment.

The second place my mind went with all of this was where he was not at all crazy. He was totally sane, and people were after him. This guy was part of some sort of espionage agency and had just gone through hell and now needs to hide out somewhere random where he won't be found. That's why he appeared somewhat dirty.

I could just picture some spy on some awesome intense mission where he gets captured and escapes torture only to find his way to my hotel for a moment of refuge, but it would not last because some James Bond style villain and his goons were after this guy. Soon my lobby would be full of them but this guy, whose name is probably Mike, saves the day. That is a total Mike thing to do after all.

But let's jump back to reality. Neither of these things happened. He will however continue to be referred to as Mike.

Here is what really happened:

I was going through the motions and getting my work done when not long into this I was getting phone calls at the desk from Mike's room.

I would answer, "Guest services how may I help you." And time and time again he would just hang up the phone as soon as I answered with that.

It happened over and repeatedly. Which got old fast.

On top of these shenanigans Mike was also making a lot of noise in his room. He was staying on the first floor but still he was down the hall in a room and the fact that I could hear him all the way down at the desk was saying something about his volume.

Naturally, I had guests calling with noise complaints. I kept getting them. I was getting them constantly. I kept trying to call his room to tell him he needed to keep it down but either would get no answer or he would answer the phone and hang up on me.

I escalated this to where I would walk down to his room and knock on the door to tell him in person. But again, was out of luck. He never answered his door for me.

Then I saw him on the camera out in the hallway walking up and down. So, I took this as an opening to confront him and tell him politely to shut the fuck up.

I walk out to the hall, "Sir! Can I speak to you for a sec?" I said.

Mike immediately begins to run the rest of the way towards his room and gets inside as quickly as he could. I even tried knocking one more time and still he did not answer.

I thought to myself, "I swear to all that is holy that if I get one more noise complaint or phone call to the desk where he just hangs up on me I am calling the police to have him removed."

My patience was wearing very thin. Beside that I did not know what kind of crazy he was. For all I know he could have violent tendencies and part of my job is to make sure this hotel is safe and secure.

I had a good 10 solid minutes of no noise at all. Then the phone rang. I looked over and saw that an outside line was calling. I had never been so happy to see that an outside line was calling me.

I answer with my normal scripted speech. Then I hear the voice on the other end say, "Hi this is police dispatch calling. Do you have a guest named Mike in room 109?"

"Why yes. Yes, I do in fact," I said.

"Well I just want to let you know that we have officers on the way to come speak to him. He called us complaining that people were after him and there was some sort of green gas seeping into his room from the vents…

Just because I must ask, have you guys had any building construction or noticed any suspicious characters around?" The dispatcher said.

"No, nothing like that," I said.

The dispatcher said, "Yeah I figured. He does not seem in his right mind. If he gives you any more trouble, please just dial 911 and we will remove him entirely."

"Well about that..." I continued, "I was actually about to call you guys as it is. I have been getting constant noise complaints on top of him calling the desk and just hanging up, and he has been loud. So, one way or another I do need him gone. I understand if you guys want to come talk to him first to see if he is okay, but I cannot keep him here tonight."

"I understand. I will let the officers know," the dispatcher said.

The call ended, and I hung up the phone. Then not 30 seconds later the phone rings again. This time it was a room calling the desk. Part of me really did not want to answer and further deal with this guy in room 109 but I did anyway because either it was someone else who needs something, or it was him and the police are on their way anyway.

I pick up the phone. Sure, as hell it was room 109 again. As irritated as I was I, for some odd reason, did not hang up.

I just answered the phone and said, "Guest services how may I help you?"

"I GOT 'EM IN THE BATHROOM!" He exclaimed.

Professional me had officially left the building. "What?" Was all I could say.

Mike frantically said, "I got them in the bathroom! They must have got in through the vents or they broke in when I left the room. I got them locked in the bathroom, but I cannot hold them off forever. The police are on their way! Tell them to hurry!"

A bit amused I asked, "Who do you have in the bathroom there?"

Mike continued on while seemingly ignoring my question, "Look! I can't hold them off forever! They can't get out before the police arrive! I have the door tied off with an extension cord!"

Now a little bit more amused I asked, "Where did you get the extension cord?"

All he said before hanging up the phone was, "Oh god! No!"

I just shrugged this off figuring it's a shame, but the police will be here soon.

Everything involving this guy was like a domino effect that night. Just one thing after another. And as such, moments after he hung up the phone, I see a sheriff deputy walk through the doors.

I smile and ask her, "Are you looking for room 109 by chance?"

She sighed and nodded her head. I directed her down the hall to where he was. Not long after, I see two city police officers enter the hotel.

Once again, I smile and cheerfully ask, "You are looking for room 109?"

Same sort of thing. They took a moment and nodded yes with a sigh. And like I had done before I directed them down the hall.

"Have fun!" I said to them as they walked away.

The domino effect of the night continued when about a minute later the deputy came back from the room shaking her head.

"I'm not dealing with that shit," she proclaimed.

Another 10 minutes of silence went by before I saw the 2 officers escort Mike up by the desk. They were trying to convince him nicely to come with them up to the hospital for a medical evaluation.

He kept trying to blow them off and carries his stuff up to the desk and said to me, "I need a new room. One where I will be much safer, and no one can break into. They're after me ya know."

I had to break the bad news to him, "Well sir honestly, there has been a ton of commotion and now police presence tonight. I'm sorry but I will not be able to keep you here tonight. Please go with them though. They want to help you and can take you somewhere safe."

Mike put his head down and said, "I understand. I apologize."

One of the officers continued trying to convince Mike to go with him, "Look just hop in the car and we will take you to the hospital. It is safe, and I'm worried about you. I just want to make sure you are okay."

Mike continued to refuse. He just kept saying that he was alright he just needs to keep going.

The officers pulled him aside and said, "Look, we really have been trying to be nice here but now we just need to spell it out for you... You do not seem in your right mind and have admitted to us that you were speaking with people who were not there and seeing things that were not there. So now, one way or another we need to take you to the hospital. So, you can ride with us or in an ambulance."

Mike puts his head down again and holds back tears, "Well I guess I will go with you guys."

He then gets into the back of the police car and they drive off. I never saw him again after that.

He really did seem normal...

YOU JUST CAN'T DO IT HERE

Sometimes if you need something done you just have to do it yourself. Even if you don't particularly want to. Such a thing is what happened to me that night.

This record of misadventure is not long but it is still funny, so I am going to tell it.

I was working until 11pm alone one evening as I had done so many times before. The time was nearing 11 which seems to be the perfect time for some sort of oddity to take place. The night auditor had called to say they were running late as well.

Between guest requests and phone calls I was trying to wrap up my evening to leave quicker once the night auditor would arrive.

I had already removed my tie and undone the top two buttons of my uniform shirt. I was very much ready to leave.

I was standing there contemplating whether to take my dress shoes off and switch into some tennis shoes. I was seriously ready to leave.

The pool at the hotel closed at 11pm. Being as it was nearing time I glanced over at the cameras to see if anyone was still in the pool or not.

I saw that the only people in the pool area at all were some couple sitting in the hot tub. I figured I would give them until the lights turn off in the pool to kick them out if they weren't out by the time the pool closes. Majority of the time I will extend this courtesy to people anyway.

Following this thought I took a call and made a reservation for the person who was calling. It was now 11 pm.

I looked over and the pool lights were still on. They would normally shut off about 5 minutes after 11 or so. Something was off though. I noticed out of the corner of my eye some movement that I could swear was not there before.

I walked over to the camera screen. I looked down and saw the same couple still in the hot tub. Except this time, they were both nude and having sex.

Like I said it was 11pm and my replacement was running late. I was the only employee currently in the building at all. And being as this is all on our security camera, I now must walk down there and tell them to stop.

I take a breath and then grab the keys. I walk down to the pool. Maybe this was just due to not knowing anything about these people or how they will react to me kicking them out of the hot tub but walking down there felt like what I can only imagine walking the green mile is like.

It was like for that moment time sort of slowed to a crawl. I was totally tunnel vision focusing in on the door to the pool area. I walked down there in this vortex of ambivalence. "Why does this shit have to happen when I am here," I repeatedly thought. Eventually I would reiterate this thought so much that I found myself saying it out loud.

I paused at the pool door. "I really hope they don't flip shit at me when I tell them they need to go to their room," I said.

I opened the door and took my time walking in and down towards the hot tub. The hot tub is somewhat tucked away and that combined with where they were in the hot tub and the fact that they were obviously preoccupied, made it so they did not notice me walk in.

I walk right up to them and stop and say, "Well this can't get any more awkward than it already is."

This comment was met with a small shriek from the woman as the man she was with pushed her off him and said, "Oh shit."

I said to them, "Look guys... I really don't care what you do. But you can't do it here."

They both looked freaked out and understandably so. The man looked asked me, "Are you gonna kick us out?!"

"Of the pool area yes," I said, "It is closing time for it anyway and I can't have you guys having sex in the hot tub."

The woman replied, "Are you gonna kick us out of the hotel though?"

I told her, "No. Not at all. You guys don't seem like creepy weirdos and like I said, I really don't care what you do... You just can't do it here."

I brought over their swimsuits which had been flung across the pool floor and a couple towels. I then said, "I'll give you guys a few minutes."

Simultaneously they both said, "Okay."

I did feel the need to point out something. "Just so you guys know," I said pointing at the security camera that faces the hot tub, "That is a working security camera. That's how I caught you guys."

I felt the need to be totally candid with them being as they were being more candid with me than they probably realized or wanted to be.

I rehashed to them that I would give them a few minutes. They just nodded their heads with their eyes still wide.

I walked back to the desk to find the night auditor just arriving. Of course, they had to arrive just as I had this situation wrapped up.

THE GHOST EMPLOYEE

Do you like ghost stories? You know, an ancient curse being broken, a creepy 1970's style house with shitty former residents, the black guy who always dies first, ancient Native American burial grounds, Stephen King, and the laughter of children with no children in sight? Well this isn't one of those stories.

I was at home one evening when I received a phone call.

I was scheduled to work the next morning and was getting a call from my coworker Sarah. Who apparently was having an issue with a guest that she needed to forewarn me about.

I answer the phone and she begins to inform me, "Hey! Sooo… You're going to be getting a complaint about me in the morning."

"Um… Okay?" I said.

Sarah continued, "So he comes to check in and is just angry from the start. I was trying to be nice. I really was, but he was just such an asshole. Then he gets up to his room and then comes back down and starts complaining about everything. Like there wasn't enough coffee in the room or like he didn't like the bed or wanted more than one shampoo up there and I should have told him and blah blah blah."

I asked Sarah, "Uh, okay. Why is he going to be complaining about you though?"

Sarah said, "Because he is a giant asshole and at first I was trying to be nice but after a while it just became more and more stupid and he became more and more of an asshole and there is only so much I can take so I was pretty well checked out of this conversation before it was over and that pissed him off more."

I told her, "Okay well I will just be ready to deal with him in the morning then. I'm going to get some sleep though, so I can actually function and handle his shit."

The call ended, and I got a bit of sleep before my alarm woke me up and I had to get ready for work.

I walked into work and everything seemed so quiet and peaceful inside. I knew this day was going to be ruined. I even wore a tie in preparation for this guy I was going to have to deal with. Not because I wanted to seem more professional. I wore a tie in case I needed to strangle him.

The morning went on without issue at first. I had been working there long enough at this point to know that nothing good (especially a seemingly nice day) will ever last.

A good 3 hours had passed, and then it happened. I looked up to see coming down the hall was a rather upset looking man.

To this day I don't know what I find more amusing; his comically angry look on his face or that his wispy comb over kept wafting back and forth and he stomped forward towards the desk.

He comes up to the desk but before he spoke he cocked his head back slightly and bulged his eyes out at me. I wasn't sure if he was trying to use some sort of non-verbal communication to portray his dissatisfaction or peer into my soul.

He then said to me, "I had a serious problem with one of the people who works here last night when I checked in."

I realized this must be the guy who I was warned about. And being as he was not curled up into a ball chanting "existence is pain" while crying and only seeing darkness all around him… It was also apparent that if he was trying to peer into my soul that he certainly failed.

"I'm sorry sir. What exactly happened?" I asked.

This guy then took a deep breath and let out a sigh before exclaiming, "I came to check in last night. The woman at the desk was horrible. I first had to wait in line to be checked in. She didn't even waive me up past everyone and I am an elite member of your rewards program I will have you know. Then upon checking me in she asked to see my photo ID! Isn't it enough that I am an elite member?! I was just treated horribly. Then to make matters worse I get up to my room and there is only 1 shampoo for me and only 3 packs of coffee for me. I require at least 2 shampoo bottles and at least 4 packs of coffee! I am not a commoner! It was just awful! Then after all that I complained to her about everything not being up to par and after a while it was just like she didn't even care! How dare she!"

I really do not know even where to begin with this guy's rant he just went on. I mean talk about first world problems. You aren't a "commoner"? Fuck you man! You're just as pathetic as anyone else you come across! I would argue even more so because you hold yourself in such elitism!

Why don't you try having a job where you have to put up with people, like yourself, who think they are soooooo much better than everyone and nothing is ever good enough for them berating you like it's that person's job to make you feel so much better about being a pathetic piece of shit of a human being. All the while being underpaid and underappreciated.

The nice thing about having the medium of printed word is I can say what I have always wanted to say to people such as that but never did out of fear of losing my job.

I still needed to respond with something. I typical phoned in apology would not do. Not just for him but for me either. This guy was way too much of an asshat. I had to say something good.

Then it dawned on me what I should say…

I asked him, "If I may ask, who were you speaking to last night? You said it was a she, but I am trying to remember if any of our female staff were even at the desk last night."

Angrily he said, "Oh it was most certain a woman! Her name was Sarah! She was just awful!"

I gave him a look of confusion. Then asked, "Sarah? Um… Are you sure their name was Sarah?"

He said, "Oh I am quite certain! I wrote it down and everything!" Then began to describe Sarah in perfect detail.

I gave him a frightened and confused look and said, "Okay that cannot be. I really don't know how you could have talked to Sarah… She uh… She wasn't exactly working last night…"

This angered him more. "Are you calling me a liar?!" He said.

I responded to him, "No sir! Not at all! I know who Sarah is… It's just that… There is no way she could have been working…"

He cut me off to say, "No! Stop this nonsense! She was here! I saw her!"

That is when I finished the job and said, "Sir I really want to help you. I am truly sorry that your experience here was not up to par so far sir… It's just that… Sarah… The one you were speaking to… I know who you are talking about. And… Sarah died about 5 years ago." I said while holding back tears to portray fake sadness.

I could physically see his demeanor change. He turned white as I have ever seen anyone turn.

He asked, "Are you kidding me?"

I said in a very sad depressed voice, "No. She died coming to work. That is why this is all so weird."

I could hear his heart beating in his chest. He managed to get yet another shade whiter as his eyes grew larger. He walked off in silence. The next morning, he checked out early.

Yeah maybe doing something like that makes me a terrible person, but you laughed. Don't lie. You thought that was just as funny as I did.

CREEPY WALMART GUY

So, there I was… Walking into work that fateful day… Little did I know that day would be the beginning a near year long ordeal.

I walk into work and pass by my supervisor at the time, Kristine, who told me to hurry up and clock in, so I could hear the crazy new shit we now are dealing with.

So, I clock in and make my way to the back office to hear what new weird shit we are now dealing with. In my head I was imagining that there was a dead body or heist or something. I was sadly disappointed to learn that once again my imagination was not reality.

In this short debriefing I was told about a man we would come to call Creepy Walmart Guy…

This asshole was calling every hotel in town from a blocked number, and only speaking to women. He would just hang up one men without saying a word. This guy would call just to be creepy and harass the female staff at various hotels.

When he first began to undertake this creepy venture of his at my hotel he spoke to a coworker of mine. She answered the phone to give our standard opening we are supposed to give everyone.

Creepy Walmart guy responded in an eerie sort of sultry voice saying, "Hey… Is there a Walmart nearby?"

My coworker not thinking anything of this thus far just said, "Well it's not right by us but you could probably drive there in about 5 minutes or so."

Unbeknownst to her this was leading right into this plan. I refuse to call it a master plan because there really isn't much to it. I mean, where is there not a Walmart nearby? I could be stranded in the desert somewhere and still find a Walmart.

Creepy Walmart Guy continued, "Oh good. I'm looking for some little girl's tights. I'm taking my daughter out to dinner and I want her looking really good for me…" He just kept on with the creepy pedophile shit until he got hung up on.

This is what I came to work to have dumped on me. I was just imagining what this guy must look like. I can just see him now. He probably has a Vincent Price mustache and slicked back hair, but Vincent Price was awesome, and this guy is totally not awesome. Not to mention this creepy wide-eyed asshole wouldn't be using pomade to slick back his hair; He would be using used Crisco. In my mind's eye he, for apparent reason, has giant thunder thighs and varicose veins as well, and of course he sits in a closet surrounded by old Better Homes and Gardens magazines.

One night he called rather late and spoke to my coworker Morgan. After he began with his opening line she recognized who was calling and responded with, "It fucking burned down!" And of course, then just hung up on that douchebag. Which of course is hilarious. You all should be laughing right now.

After being told the whole story which also involved the fact that the police had been notified and he has been harassing every hotel in town, I just gave this mortified, disgusted look on my face. Both at what was going on and my mental picture of this creep. I really do not know which was more horrifying.

I was given instruction to call the police or just call the detective who had been assigned to the case directly should this guy call, come by, or any new information arise about him. Creepy Walmart Guy went so far as to start to memorize names of people at different hotels and when they were usually at work, so he could call them and be a creepy stalker. Pretty fucked up right?

We did come to learn that hotels in various other cities were getting calls from this guy. Started to make me wonder if he really had nothing to do but sit around and find various hotels in the state to call and harass the women at. What a fucking loser.

Time proceeded to go on and Creepy Walmart Guy continued his barrage of creepy phone calls. There were many times all the men who worked at the desk were very certain that we had answered when he called because upon answering we would see it was a private number and as soon as any of us said anything the person on the other end would disconnect the call without saying a word.

Over the months there seemed to be this ebb and flow with his creepy phone calls. These phone calls never deviated from what he first began with. He always began by asking "Is there a Walmart nearby?" before continuing as expected with the usual. It's almost as though he had this scripted or something.

During one of his especially long breaks we began to wonder if maybe he was done calling. Maybe he had got arrested or better yet fed to a pack of rabid wolves.

Sure enough, our extended break was cut short and Creepy Walmart Guy was back at it again. He had called so much that we had this giant manila file on him. And now he appears to not only be back but stepping up his game.

Our general manager was instructed by the detective in charge of the investigation to do our best to keep him on the phone if we can and take down the date and time before calling the police to make it easier for the police department to unblock the phone number.

Maybe a couple of months after that I find out through the grapevine that one of the other hotels in the area was able to get the company they go through for cable, phone, and internet to go through their phone records and unblock the number he was calling from. The number was from somewhere on the other side of the country. What made all of this still difficult was that he was using a prepaid phone so there was no name tied to it.

I came to work the next day after hearing that news and immediately told my supervisor what I had learned. She in turn told me I needed to call that detective guy and give him this information. Which I figured would ultimately be the case but still wanted to run this by her as well.

I never did meet this detective in person. I can only assume he was tall, slender, with a widow's peak and aviators who wears jeans with his suit and cowboy boots as he rides around in an old Buick like a character from a cop drama in the 80's. At least that is what I want to be the case because it is probably a lot more interesting than who this guy really is.

I called the detective on his cell phone number he gave us. He answered, and I explained who I was and gave him all the information I was given as you may have guessed. Or at least I hope this comes as no shock to you.

Well he just plainly responded to me saying, "Yeah, we actually already knew about all that. I'm going to be perfectly honest with you, this is not just some prank caller. This is actually part of a much larger investigation involving several law enforcement agencies across the country."

"Holy shit!" Was all I could think to say.

He said, "Yeah. No joke. And I will say this… Without giving away too much away as some is still classified… In the past 48 hours he has made 837 phone calls to properties across the country."

So not only is this guy creepy and weird and gross but we are also looking at someone who literally has no life. Instead of sitting in his parent's basement and playing games online he is sitting in what I assume to be a rat hole apartment with a phone and a shitload of phone numbers that he calls daily. There really is no substance or purpose to this individual's existence.

This guy needed to be brought down. Not just by police though. I mean sure he is creepy and gross and needs to be thrown in jail, but I needed to ruin this guy's day somehow. I decided that I just had to get this guy to talk to me on the phone just, so I could ruin this for him. Of course, this would take some thought and planning.

I recalled a line from the movie "Death to Smoochie" which Robin Williams and Edward Norton. This line was from a scene where Robin Williams' character called Edward Norton's character and quickly rattled off one of the most epic threats I had ever heard. My plan was to first memorize this line and once I can find a way to get this guy on the phone talking to me I would just spout it off.

Of course, the question now was how the hell could I get him to talk to me on the phone?

Time continued, and we hit another slow point with his calls. We had wondered if he finally gave up. It had at least seemed that way.

Well one evening I was working with my coworker, Gina, when as luck would have it there was a phone call. And I am sure you are all aware that it was Creepy Walmart Guy calling.

So, the phone rings and Gina, without thinking, answered the phone.

She opens with the usual line. Upon hearing him say, "Hey Gina, is there a Walmart nearby?" Her eyes just got huge and she covers the mouthpiece and said to me, "It's fucking Creepy Walmart Guy!"

I said to her, "Holy shit! Keep him talking! The longer he is on the phone the easier it will be for the police to track him down!"

Then in the milliseconds following it hit me. My plan for getting him on the phone with me was right there, and it was happening in real time. This opportunity was too good to pass up.

I told Gina to go call the police but hand me the phone. I would cover the mouthpiece and listen to him talk. Every so often though I would direct her to say something to him. Of course, I was leaving out the part of me looking for my opening to just ruin his whole fucking day.

We are going along with everything as I had planned in that moment. Every so often I am having her say yes or no or maybe a quick phrase or sentence into the phone just to keep this guy talking.

You could tell he was getting a bit concerned with the slight delay in her responses but alas he continued. One he started getting creepy with all the pedophile shit I thought this would be the perfect time to interject.

Right at a pause I opened my mouth and recited that glorious line from "Death to Smoochie" and said, "You better grow eyes in the back of your fucking head you horned piece of shit because I'm not gonna sleep until worms are crawling out your foam rubber ass. I'm going on safari motherfucker! SA-FAR-I!"

There was a quick pause on the phone. I could tell he held on for a second but wasn't saying anything. Then he just hung up abruptly.

A couple weeks after this we found out that Creepy Walmart Guy was arrested. Law enforcement agencies were able to ping his phone signal off a cell tower that was 2 blocks away from his apartment. His apartment was full of phone books and stacks of papers with phone numbers and names.

While I would never condone his behavior; I will say that due to the sheer volume of phone calls he made and as many places as me made them, I am sure at least some of you reading this had some sort of encounter with this same guy regardless of the nickname you may or may not have given him. So, if you didn't already know, he got arrested and I hope this story was both entertaining but also disturbing with the flashbacks it gave you.

DOCTOR WHO?

The front desk is a border town. Sometimes this town is a peaceful village of fellow travelers. Sometimes it's a demilitarized zone between two warring factions. You never quite know who you are going to interact with upon meeting someone, in that border town, and you never quite know what their choice of actions will be until they do it.

Most of the people are fairly "normal" and "cookie cutter" in that everything is direct and straightforward and your interactions with them will be kept short and neither of you will make much (if any) of an impact on each other.

Then there are those of whom which you interact that make you question the fate of humanity.

This story is about the latter of the two.

It was an early morning when our tale first began to eventuate. This morning would be the beginning of everlasting nonsense and drivel I would not soon forget.

I had walked down to the pool briefly that morning. Upon walking back to the desk, I see a woman, just standing there, like she was beamed in from someplace sad and claustrophobic. She was most likely in her 50s, frizzy brown hair, and wearing a heavy puffy coat which I found strange being as this was during the summer.

I walk up and see her writing on a piece of paper like she was in a hurry. Then she slides the piece of paper across the desk.

I begin to pick up the pace to help her. I raise the volume of my voice a bit and say, "I'll be right with you ma'am."

She stops me before I can make my way behind the desk. She waved her hand a bit at me. Talking fast as though in a hurry she said, "Oh no no no. It's quite alright. I just noticed you were walking down the hall and I didn't know if you were going to be gone long and I just wanted to leave you a note because I had a reservation for tonight and it looks like I am just going to keep going so I won't be needing to stay tonight after all and just needed you to cancel tonight for me. My name is Dr. Karla Anderson."

I told her, "Okay, I will get this taken care of."

She left, and I came around the desk. I looked at the piece of paper she was scribbling on. It read "Dr. Karla Anderson- Please cancel tonight".

I could not have been down at the pool for more than one minute, and her note was much shorter than her long winded and rather rushed rant of what she needed.

This was not the first time a guest had been in such a situation. I figured she was an in-house guest of mine who was in a hurry out the door and wanted to, in a roundabout sort of way, tell me she was leaving a day early. I would find myself to be incorrect though.

I was looking around for reservation but could not seem to find it. I eventually changed the dates, so I could see everything past, present, future.

Then I saw it. There it was staring right at me. She had made a reservation for the night before. Since she had done so and not arrived the night before her reservation went to no show and she was charged accordingly. And now here she is, the next morning, wanting to cancel for the night before. No, that is not how this all works.

So basically, instead of showing up on the day she made the reservation for, she decided to show up the morning after and expect us to just travel back in time to just cancel her reservation. Easy peasy lemon squeezy.

Unfortunately, my TARDIS and Flux Capacitor are not operational. Nor do I have enough road to get up to 88 miles per hour. This was just not going to happen. She is still going to be charged.

I let my bosses know what was going on just in case she tried to call to say she cancelled in hopes of a refund. They agreed that she should be charged.

Naturally as expected she called about two days later to bemoan and complain of being charged for the reservation she cancelled even though the day after is far beyond anyone's cancellation policy.

Karla had the audacity to say, "The man I spoke to the other morning said he would cancel my reservation without any charges and that since I'm a doctor I would even get a free night in the future!"

In no way shape or form did I or would I ever tell her any of this. She was completely full of shit. There is no way she would not be charges like I said, and we are not just going to give out free nights to people just because they are a doctor. This just does not happen. And after a long back and forth argument with my boss she finally got the hint that her refund was just not going to happen.

About a week went by with no word from her. As expected after that week there is a new reservation for Dr. Karla Anderson for three nights.

I was not the one to check her in thankfully. My boss did. She, of course, threw a huge fuss at check in. She began to dispute her previous charges from the week before.

Karla was swearing up and down again that I promised she would not be charged and would also get that free night in the future for being a doctor, and to make things all the much more interesting she claimed that when she called to speak to the manager that he agreed that she should get her refund and free night as well. I mean… She's a doctor after all.

My manager said something to the effect of, "Well actually that was me you spoke to and no, I at no time said you would be getting a refund or a free night for that matter."

I wish I could have been there to see the look on her face. It must have been priceless. This made me begin to question whether she was a doctor or not.

She was sadly staying for three nights so there was no way that would be the end of this for her. She was way off the deep end and well invested in her insanity.

The first time I saw her during this stay of hers I was hoping she would not recognize me. However, the universe had other plans for me.

I saw her floating around the breakfast bar looking almost disoriented. It was as if she maybe had one too many but not so many that she had to hold onto the floor, so she would not fall off. Like sure she was intoxicated but she still had some lucidity. Although the horrible part about all of this is that I am certain this was sober her.

Karla was wearing a black turtleneck, a red sweater vest over that, and khakis. She just needed a loud speaker and a soap box to stand on while she announces to everyone everywhere that she needs to speak to their manager.

From across the way she locked onto me with her lifeless dilated pupils. There was no escaping her nonsensical bullshit now.

She forcefully points at me and says, "You!" before making her way towards me.

I felt like I had the angel and the devil on my shoulders. One was saying "Just stay professional! Don't be an asshole!" and the other was saying "Go on! Do it! Tell her off! Tell her how annoying she is and that she is a prevaricating sack of 3-day old moldy diarrhea!" It was honestly hard to tell which one of them was the benevolent and which of them was the malevolent one.

She makes her way over to me to say, "You! You promised me a refund and a free night!"

I had to really bite my tongue. I am surprised blood was not dripping out.

When I did decide to speak I did in fact decide to try to stay professional and keep everything short. I said, "No ma'am. I sure did not. Please if you have any concerns feel free to speak with our general manager in the morning."

Continuing her retort, she said, "I spoke with all the managers and they agreed! Why? Why wouldn't you stick to your word! I'm a doctor! Just tell me what is going on! If you need to look me up again my name is Dr. Karla Anderson."

Her need to continuously point out that she was a doctor in conjunction with her mental state being questionable at best; I was wondering more and more if she was in fact a doctor or maybe she just played one on T.V. But probably not even that because she is stupid and there is no way she would be cool enough. Which is saying something because some of those shows will hire anyone.

I really did not want to get into any argument with her at the time. I just wanted to work in peace and it was disturbing enough to me that I had to breathe the same air as her.

To end our current interaction, I just repeated myself verbatim, "No ma'am. I sure did not. Please if you have any concerns feel free to speak with our general manager in the morning."

She took a moment to process what I was saying. It really did not make complete sense with what she was saying, and I would imagine even she could recall that I had said this prior word for word.

Karla's brow furrowed, and her eyes crossed a bit as she gave me this open mouth frown. She kept this look for a moment without saying anything.

I said nothing, but silently kept my mantra of, "Don't break the awkward silence" going.

Eventually she muttered something under her breath and walked away. This of course making me the victor.

The next day Karla and thankfully did not interact. I did see her in passing but we did not speak to one another.

I kept thinking about how I was not entirely convinced that she was a doctor. She was way too weird and crazy. Sure, I found her annoying and had a bias, but I could not accept the fact that she contributes to the health and wellbeing of others in any way.

I looked at the company on her reservation. The only company I could find with such a name was some sort of electronics company. This was not a definite that I was correct in my assumption that Karla Anderson was not in fact Karla Anderson, M.D. but it was indeed a large amount of evidence in my favor.

Time went on and the supposed "Dr. Anderson" was still sure she was getting a discount, free night, and a refund. Much of this weighed heavily on her being a doctor. She really liked pointing this out.

Her need to continuously point out kept giving me this festering thought that she was lying about being a doctor. I mean she was obviously completely bat shit crazy and kept lying about everything else.

Late one-night Karla began to lurk around the hallways like the undead. She had her arms mostly stretched out and was just sort of walking around aimlessly and awkwardly with her eyes darting around all over the place. It is quite likely she was on some good drugs.

Eventually Karla did enough lurking that she found herself at the desk standing in front of me. There was another moment of pause before she spoke. I imagine this was her training to gain some lucidity about where she was at the time, and possibly who she was.

With forced authority Karla said to me, "Excuse me, I don't know if you remember me but I'm Dr. Karla Anderson. I am staying here for a few nights and you promised me that my stay would be free because there was a mix up and I am just coming by because I needed to make sure you made my stay free. You promised me my stay would be free."

There really was no way of sugar coating anything with her at all anymore. She was either stupid, crazy, or both. Regardless she would not stop bothering me.

My face started to turn red as I said, "No, I did not offer you a free night or nights. In fact, no one did. You will be charged for your stay just like everyone else. Neither I or anyone else including all the way up to our general manager has offered you anything."

She had this look of despair on her face like she just watched someone punch her grandparents. Considering this woman being of a slightly older generation this would suggest someone was punching a couple of corpses.

Karla, holding back her rage, said, "That is a lie! I was promised! I'm a doctor! Don't you understand that? I'm a doctor!"

I just could not contain my skepticism any longer. I refused to believe someone this crazy can contribute to the health and welfare of another human being. I had just had it with this woman.

I just let it out and said to Karla, "You know what? I don't think you are actually a doctor."

Karla became flabbergasted and threw her arms around and began to breathe heavily. A bead of sweat started to run down her face.

"Excuse me! I went to medical school! I am a doctor! I save lives!" She said.

To which I responded, "No. Just no. I don't buy it for a moment. I have never met a doctor who, not only was as mentally unstable, but also lied about literally everything and had to continuously point it out to everyone. I call bullshit."

Karla gave me the same flabbergasted look and arm animation as she did prior. To be honest, there was a part of me that could not believe I was just saying it, but as it came out I thought to myself, "All right. Let's do this. This is happening. I'm saying this."

She then yelled, "Well fine! If you don't believe me the go ahead and call the state board of health and see what they have to say! Go on! I dare you!"

I grinned and said, "Okay! I will then!" as I pulled up the number on Google.

I then called on speaker phone and gave them all her info. She was not actually a doctor. I was right.

Once I hung up the phone Karla, if that was indeed her real name, looked at me like she was trying to set me on fire with her mind. Then she muttered something under her breath and ran off.

While I was not surprised that we never did see or hear from her again I was very surprised that she did not make any sort of complain to my manager. I guess I won that war.

FIRE ALARM

Having to evacuate an entire hotel during a fire alarm is never any fun. Trust me I have done it. We just had to be sold out that night too.

Not only was every room occupied but most people were trying to cram more people into each room than what the room could safely hold. There was a constant flow of people throughout the hotel. So much so that we had extra people on and we still were struggling to keep up with the needs of guests.

Everyone staying that night needed absolutely everything. On top of this we couldn't keep clean towels down at the pool for anything.

I felt like I needed riot gear that day just to deal with people. Not because they were forming some sort of mob, but because I was just sick of them.

Murphy's law is a real thing. Just as the hotel could not get anymore chaotic, this shit happened...

I was walking back to the desk after delivering something to a guest at their room. I had been running around so much I was beginning to sweat. I had taken off my tie and rolled up my sleeves.

I was right over by the elevators when I heard that horrible, annoying, potentially lifesaving noise. The fire alarm had been pulled.

I quickly looked around for signs of smoke or flames. I saw nothing. I made my way towards the desk. On my way I was telling people where to go outside and if they needed help locating their family members to see me at the desk.

I got to the desk and watched as many people were walking outside. The maintenance manager and a housekeeper were peeking around for signs of smoke or fire and not seeing anything.

Seeing as no one found any sign whatsoever of a fire, which then leads me to think that some asshole child thought it would be funny to pull the fire alarm. Still though, due to standard operating procedure, I needed to make sure that everyone was safe and wait for the fire department to call. No one who had the alarm code to shut off the alarm was on property that day either.

Guest's kept approaching me at the desk and with very irritated tones of voices kept asking me why exactly the fire alarm was going off as if the answer was not already in the question.

I was getting really annoyed with people continuously asking this. Not asking where they need to go outside but why the alarm is going off or when I am going to fix it. I was incredibly tempted to just tell them that I pulled the fire alarm because my life's goal is to fuck up their whole vacation.

A woman from the fire department's dispatch calls, "Hi, this is Julie. I am with the dispatch. We see you have an alarm going off."

I replied, "Yes ma'am. The alarm is going off but there is no sign of smoke or fire anywhere."

"Well that at least is good news," She said, "Is everyone out of the building?"

To which I said, "As far as I can see, there are a few remaining people making their way out right now but other than that just us here at the desk are left. Although I don't have the code to turn off the alarm"

Julie told me, "That is good people seem to be out. When the fire department arrives, they can shut off the alarm. Just be on the lookout for smoke or flames still and maybe double check on people. If you see anything that indicates fire just call 911."

I got off the phone and helped our maintenance staff double check that everyone had left and that there was indeed no sign of fire. They shared my thoughts that some shithead kid pulled the alarm just to be a dick.

I had made my way back to the desk. The fire department at just arrived. They went to shut off the alarm and make their way through the building.

At this most spectacular time, the phone rang...

Upon answering the phone, I was greeted by a woman who was the corporate office for a certain major airline who will remain nameless.

You see, we had a flight crew staying with us that night and this woman was with the division of their corporate office that deals with setting up their lodging when they travel. I will never forget her. Her name was Bertha. I found this fitting because I imagine she looks like an old saddle bag or a dumpster behind a slaughterhouse.

After my standard greeting and her introducing herself she then continued to open the floodgates of bullshit known as her mouth.

Bertha said to me, "Well you see sir, we have a flight crew staying with you and we just received a call from the captain who is staying on the top floor in your establishment. He is claiming that there is in fact a fire alarm going off in the building right now. Can you confirm this?"

At first, I was a bit puzzled by why she would be calling to ask about the fire alarm but figured maybe they must get in touch with the corporate office somehow in these situations. It did seem logical to me.

I said to Bertha, "Yes ma'am. We are experiencing the fire alarm right now."

Bertha's intonation changed. She switched over from sounding profession to sounding annoyed and smug.

With her new-found articulation she said, "Well you see sir, pilots are required law to get a certain number of hours of sleep before flying a plane. The captain is now worried with the disturbance of the fire alarm that he will not be able to get the required amount of sleep and is considering switching hotels for the evening. Now, do you want to tell me why exactly the fire alarm is going off? It is disturbing the captain."

I found this line of questioning odd. I understand he needs sleep and wants sleep and all that, but why is she in any way wondering why the fire alarm is going off? This usually indicates some sort of emergency.

Maybe it was all the people annoying me that day, maybe it was the fire alarm, maybe it was her shitty attitude, maybe it was her stupid question, or maybe it was just a combination everything, but I just felt like I should just be blunt about all this.

I opened my mouth and said, "Well, let's think about this with logic for a moment... Why on earth would a fire alarm be going off? There couldn't potentially be a fire or something. That would just be too logical. I think the real question is why he is sitting in his room on the top floor with windows that don't even open and not evacuating with the rest of the guests?"

I know I said there was no sign of smoke or flames but that does not mean that there wasn't a fire somewhere in the building. Not to mention you want to treat any fire alarm as the real thing especially if you are sitting in your room on the top floor.

Bertha had to pause for a moment. I could hear breathing on the other line like she was trying to not blow up.

Bertha finally spoke continuing her pompous attitude saying, "Look. I don't think you understand the gravity of the situation. He needs sleep to legally be able to fly, and right now is wanting to switch hotels. Now are you certain there is a fire? I just don't understand why this alarm has been triggered."

Remaining blunt with her I said, "I don't understand the gravity of the situation?! Your goddamn captain is sitting on the top floor of the hotel in his room meanwhile everyone else has evacuated, including the rest of the flight crew I might add. Now I have you acting like wonderfully snobby wondering why a FIRE ALARM is going off?! Look, he can stay up in his room and risk his life if he wants. Should he want to go to a hotel we will gladly take him there even though that will cut into even more of his sleep time."

Even after my angry rant she still did not seem to get my use of logic and reason. It was as if she did not listen at all to a word I had said.

"Sir, I'm going to need to know why the fire alarm is going off," Bertha said.

"Because obviously there is an emergency situation and he does need to evacuate with everyone else," I said.

"Sir, I'm gonna need to know why the fire alarm is going off," Bertha said.

I really wanted to reach through the phone and set fire to her desk. That may be the only way for her to truly understand. Or she still would not get it and just sit there until she dies in the all-consuming flames. Either way I would find satisfaction in the outcome.

I once again said, "Because obviously there is an emergency situation and he does need to evacuate with everyone else."

This conversation repeated itself for a bit longer. I finally had had it. I said to Bertha, "I'm hanging up now." And just hung up on her.

As suspected the fire marshal deemed that some kid had indeed pulled the fire alarm as some sort of prank.

Eventually the pilot decided to stay at the hotel about 2 blocks away. We gladly gave him a ride over there. The rest of the flight crew did not want to move with him. They were more than content with staying.

I was rather pleased to overhear one of the other members of the flight crew say to the captain when he asked if they wanted to leave with him, "You're acting like a child."

Fast forward to the next day. I got to work and was called into my general manager's office.

Upon walking in there I was greeted with him saying, "Oh my fucking god!"

He goes on to tell me that the same exact woman called to not only complain about me but the fire alarm. Not only did he back me up, but he had pretty much the exact conversation I had with her all the way up to the point of which that he hung up on her.

Maybe misery really does love company because I was laughing hard when I heard that. It still amuses me to think about.

THREE AND A HALF FAMILIES

Have you ever wondered if you were on some sort of hidden camera show? You know when you experience something that just makes you wonder how this could possibly be real and just makes you wonder when the guy with the camera is going to pop out of the bushes and surprise you, like a jovial mugger? I know I have had that feeling. Except this did not happen for me on some day where I was out and about. This feeling was spread over about a month.

So, there were these three families that came to stay at my hotel for about a month or so. They had this family-run business that kept all of them traveling and a lot of money coming in.

The families all seemed to intermarry among the three families and having their creepy inbred children that would eventually become their workforce. It was like "The Hills Have Eyes" but with vagabonds. Or the beginning of a Kentucky-only Father's Day card.

First a couple of them came to check in. They said they were in town working. Then suddenly, their entire extended families start showing up, like zombies to a Phish concert.

My entire hotel was filled with the people from "The Hills Have Eyes."

Being as much of the bullshit the staff endured at the hands of these families was the same thing every day; I will try to avoid being long winded and just share the more memorable experiences of these families and their corn children.

I should first expand on who they were:

These families had this sort of traveling business that was most likely snake-oil based. They would take contracts from pretty much anywhere they could get them and pack up their whole families and live out of their vehicles and hotel rooms just traveling around taking various jobs.

Well this company they ran was anything but reputable. You see, after looking them up on the Better Business Bureau's website to find their business has an F rating, and if your BBB rating is in anyway relatable to Kim Kardashian's current-grade math scores, there is a problem.

Basically, what we were able to dig up was that they would take these jobs around the country and would get paid, do the job part way, and then take off. Like carnies without the fat-soaked elephant ears. Or, fat-soaked without any ears. Whatever. You see some strange crap in my line of work. Anyways, then they would make sure to not return to that area to work until the two-year warranties they give their clients had expired. Their F rating was from all such activity and their numerous unanswered complaints people had filed.

They were con artists. Traveling ones at that. I felt like I had traveled back 100 years and was meeting with snake oil salesman. Unlike most Appalachian snake handlers, however, these three families had somehow not killed themselves under the pressure of Darwinian natural selection. Hence it fell that they landed on my desk.

They owned this traveling construction business and traveled about the country doing horrible jobs for people all while intermarrying and having inbred children.

Once these people show up they would not leave. They would just keep extending their stay. Now, don't get me wrong: on the one hand, money is good. But these people are obnoxious and loud and annoying, and I hate them. Cash versus sanity is a horrible conundrum to deal with.

After a while they would start to pay for each night. Everything was fine until we started having to track them down for payments.

The weeks went on and their rooms were trashed every day, the hallways were filled with dirty diapers from what I hope was their young children, but you cannot be too sure with this group, and of course late payments for their room.

I'm not joking about these trashed rooms and diaper filled halls. The housekeepers would walk in to service their rooms and it would look like Johnny Depp partied in there while a professional wrestling event went on and Frankie Muniz brought the coke. It looked like this daily and smelled like a dumpster full of potted meat.

How anybody manages to accomplish this amount of refuse and debris each day remains a great mystery.

I really don't get the diapers in the hallway thing. Not only is it just gross and causes murder rates to rise but it makes no sense. The halls in no way resemble a trash or a diaper genie. And like I said before, I can only hope it was from their small children. Due to the collective IQ of this group one cannot be too sure.

Oddly enough, one of the dirtier of them was also a giant germaphobe. Not sure how being the one responsible for creating so much filth and being a germaphobe was supposed to work but it did.

He was always showering and washing his hands and not wanting to touch anything without gloves or in some cases tongs. And of course, he never shook hands with anyone.

During their sojourn at the hotel, they had one and only one family member arrives by plane. I guess he couldn't stand to be around them for prolonged periods of time either.

My coworker, Corey, was the one who ended up giving the germaphobe, Peter, a ride up to the airport to meet his brother cousin up there.

Corey came back from this little excursion eyes wide open and a look plastered on his face like he just watched a midget who was butt ass naked with a chicken mask on trying to rob a train.

I knew something worth telling took place, so I asked Corey, "What happened?"

Corey stopped in his tracks, opened his mouth and said, "I took him up to the airport. On the way up there, he got in the car and yelled at me for not having a USB port for him, and then got on the phone with someone saying he was staying with his mom at some random hotel in another city. Then just started singing some weird ass song in like some foreign language. Like just yelling this shit out. Then he takes a bottle of water and starts pouring it on himself and tells me 'It's been a long flight.' Like what the fuck?"

So as bad as this group of them was, they had another group of extended family member that were worse.

So now that the stage has been set, let us continue down the rabbit hole and get into the real shit story.

Some weeks went by after the families had left. If I had to guess I would say they probably had to pause work to attend the weddings of their cousins with their other cousins. 'Happy Birthday Uncle Dad!' was, probably a common refrain at these annual gatherings.

Some weeks continued to pass, and we had not had to deal with any of them. By nothing short of a miracle, we were able to rid the hotel of the foul aroma. Times were truly glorious.

All good things must come to an end, however. Going through life, this is something we all hopefully learn to accept. In this industry it hits you so hard that any extreme optimist will turn into a raging cynic.

After this wonderful period without any of these families, and all genetic variability-seeking behavior restored to normal, non-family levels, one of their names pops in my arrivals screen. A black cloud of despair engulfed the hotel.

This individual unit of their families had yet to stay at the hotel. They were also far worse than their predecessors, as time inevitability proved.

While their previous family was indeed obnoxious, dirty, fetid, and with intelligence levels and mental state being questionable at best... this other part of their family was something else entirely. I would call them the worst guests ever but that would be an insult to the worst guests ever.

They were even more filthy, dirty, and disgusting. They were horribly rude and inconsiderate of literally everyone else in existence. And just to add some flavor they were also bigoted. If you took a Klan rally and made it portable with carney values, you'd get the next few weeks at my hotel.

They immediately set the tone arriving at the hotel at 10am to check in. Keep in mind this is before check-out time. If a room is open and ready to go then yes by all means they would have been able to check in, but the night before we were sold out. So, no rooms were clean and vacant that this family could check into at that time.

This was unacceptable to them. The mother figure, Molly, made it very clear that when they come to town we better be ready to take care of their every whim and desire. She had these overly entitled expectations, but a 1920s freak show family tree.

So, she threw a huge fit and we all had to be educated on how important her family really is. Which of course just makes us begrudge their very existence.

Eventually they got into their room which would turn into their makeshift home for the next while. It was not long after checking in that people had already called with noise complaints about their room.

It wasn't just like the normal sort of noise complaints where a guest might say something along the lines of, "Hey the people above us are being a bit loud. Can you ask them to keep it down please?"

It was more along the lines of, "I don't know what is going on up above me, but it sounds like they are using power tools while jumping up and down."

Or when someone said, "The people next to us are screaming nonstop at each other."

And of course, "There are children running through the halls trying to beat each other up."

All of this became the daily norm. It was completely ridiculous.

During their unfortunate time at my hotel, they were just all around terrible. One of the more infuriating things they did was each day they would put their Do Not Disturb sign on their door. Which would be fine. It really would. In fact, in this case, we would all prefer to never interact with this group of sub-humanoids. Except that they would leave their sign up but then call down to the desk later and moan and groan about not having their room serviced.

When it was clear that this was going to be a habit of theirs, it was then explained that they would not get their room serviced for as long as they had their Do Not Disturb sign up, and that they only had until noon to let us know that they would like service.

Doing this then brought about their new annoying habit of taking down their sign right before noon and then calling the desk to say they need service.

To make matters worse, the housekeepers would go up there and the room would be trashed. Just completely polluted and desecrated and would be a renewed mess each day. It was like walking into a war zone, and it smelled like moldy curry too. It was a war zone.

So, the housekeeper would go in to clean this loathsome room and Molly would refuse to leave the room while they cleaned. There she stood, curling iron in hand, the Queen of her blue-collar, inbred Narnia Kingdom. Which added further unneeded difficulties.

Of course, there is the obvious problem of her physically getting in the way of them cleaning, but Molly would take things a step further. While the housekeepers were attempting to clean up what looked to be nuclear wreckage, she would yell and scream at them until they started crying. She made some of the staff cry.

Naturally she had to be spoken to about not being a terrible person or at the very least pretend enough that there are not employees crying and not wanting to see her. We can only deal with the crying or the not wanting to see her. Together it becomes a bit of an issue.

This then led into her deciding to take things off housekeeping carts. From towels all the way up to vacuums and everywhere in between. All the while she kept her Do Not Disturb sign on the door. So now we must deal with her stealing shit and keeping a sign on her door telling housekeeping to stay out, and then putting used towels outside the door for housekeepers to find had been used to clean up piles of excrements. These people seriously shit in the towels. Like Kanye at 2am on Twitter, they went there. And doubled down.

Once again this had to be dealt with accordingly. By that I mean Molly was confronted by management and told she could not do that and had to give back the vacuum because that was theft. And should any more shit towels be found they would just be asked to leave.

She continued with taking shit off the carts and leaving her Do Not Disturb up on her door and then complaining about not getting service. It got old fast, and of course these people just would not leave. The only silver lining being that at least for now there were no shit towels in the hallway.

Being as Molly still chose not to listen and follow very simple and reasonable directions, a little note was typed up for her that was signed by our manager and slipped under her door.

This note told her that due to all these various circumstances, their family would not be receiving housekeeping service unless they call the desk each day before 11am and request it. So that way they have that hour less to screw around with the housekeeping schedule and it would just be assumed otherwise that they do not want service.

This little note did not sit well with them but oh well they can just stop being shitty people. Besides, they went along with it so that was a victory for the staff.

Somehow, they felt that an appropriate response to us angering them was to then allow their 10-year-old evil ginger son to go into the pool and throw tables and chairs around and starting fights with people.

Understandably this got him banned from the pool. Molly then caused a scene which got their whole family kicked out of the pool entirely.

The father figure in this family was almost never anywhere to be found. And when we would see the husband/father figure, whom I can only assume was one in the same person and probably somehow otherwise related.

All of this finally came to a head when our night auditor was walking up the stairs only to find five giant full black trash bags had just been thrown onto the landing and was now blocking anyone from going up or down the stairs. So, I guess in case of a fire everyone not on the ground floor can all just die. And to make matters worse, they still had a completely trashed room even after all that garbage. Their evil ginger son even went so far as to shove doughnuts into the fan in their room and then urinate in the dresser drawers.

And again, there were shit towels set outside the door in a pile of shittiness. Or people going all R Kelly on the dresser.

They needed to go. This was all too much constant bullshit from one room.

Then it happened… Everything came crashing down on them.

I was working one night until 11. No one had seen or heard from them all day, so you know they were up to something. Still we were all trying to count our blessings.

At around 9:30 pm Molly comes to the desk. And she was just seething. She looked a lot like Drew Barrymore on the cover of Firestarter. Or Drew Carey being set on fire. Either way, I had to look around for flames.

I asked her, "How can I help you?"

To which she responded, "Well I'm just shitting pissed I'll tell ya!"

Without delay I said, "Gross."

She asked, "What?"

Then I asked, "What?"

Molly continued, "Since we got here we have had nothing but trouble with the cleaning staff. They won't clean our room right and we can't never get what we need."

Not only was I very much ready for their whole family to leave, but they were going to be asked to leave very soon anyway so I figured it did not really matter what I would say to her.

I just said, "Oh… Well that's a shame."

Molly gave me a look of horror and disgust like I had just punched her grandpa in a wheelchair.

She responded, "I don't appreciate that! I don't appreciate any of this! I cannot believe that no one will just do their job!"

Once again, I just said, "Oh… Well that's a shame."

Molly paused to give me the death glare again and then said, "First no one was cleaning right. Then I get told I can't use the vacuum or have fresh towels. Then I get a letter under the door saying we won't get housekeeping unless we call the desk before noon and ask for it."

Remaining unruffled I said to Molly, "Well I mean maybe you shouldn't be treating people like shit and stealing stuff off housekeeping carts. Just a thought."

Molly began to move her hands around in frustration and became more and more animated.

She yelled, "My husband was working late today! We have been gone out of the building all day because of this and now I'm getting home to find my room wasn't being done! It doesn't matter that I didn't ask today! They should have just done it because it is their job! I will not live in a pile of filth!"

I asked her, "Are you sure about that? Because judging by the state of your guys' room each day…

I would say living in filth and squalor is just what you do."

"You're a fucking asshole! All of you are! I fucking hate this place!" Molly said before pausing to catch her breath. Then she continued, "I want to speak to the general manager right now!"

"That sounds like a great idea! Let's give him a call!" I said.

So, I called my boss Jim at home and blithely said, "Yeah so our most favorite guest ever is standing in front of me yelling and screaming and… She wants to talk to you!"

I pass the phone off to Molly who just goes off about everything she was screaming at me about. All the way down to the swearing and name calling. Which was then followed up with her saying, "I don't want to have to stay another night here!"

I could hear Jim's voice coming from the phone say with excitement, "Yeah that sounds great! Why don't you guys pack your things and prepare to leave."

Molly handed the phone back with her jaw hitting the floor and her eyes wide open. She said nothing but slowly made her way out of my presence. I could not have been happier.

That subdivision of their family was never heard from by us again. They made their absence known with a lack of shit towels in the halls. There was much rejoicing.

THESE TWO GUYS

In the many years I have worked in the hospitality industry, I have had many unforgettable moments that will live with me forever.

There was the time that a guest brought me prime rib and gave me a $20 tip because I was "doing a hell of a job" and I "don't make enough money."

But then there are the moments that happen, leaving me wondering, who the fuck raised you?

So, there I was... As so many good stories begin... I was working until 11 PM. The day was rather slow. I came into not many arrivals and there was barely any pick up either. The rates were not set very high that day on top of everything.

I was extremely bored. I was really hoping that something would cure my boredom, and sadly I got exactly what I asked for.

After much time of speaking to no one, I looked up to see two men walking in the doors. These men were traveling together and needed a room for the night. So far nothing abnormal.

One man was middle aged. I would guess in his mid-50's. The other man was probably 20 years or so younger. The older of the two men, who mentally I named Chad, was the only one to utter a word to me the whole time.

Chad looks at me with an almost empty glare and says, "I need a room."

"All right sir," I reply, "How many beds do you need?"

Still with his nearly blank stare Chad said, "I'll need two beds. How much is it?"

I went on to quote him the rate for the night for a room with two beds. This was not taken very well by him. This did in fact anger him.

Chad looked at me with an even more lifeless stare. He paused for a moment with his jaw slightly opened.

Finally, he spoke and said, "Ridiculous! Give me a lower rate! Now!"

There is a right and a wrong way to haggle. To my knowledge no one usually minds a bit of haggling with the rate. There are certain times where it just is not going to happen even if I wanted it to simply because we are way too busy, but majority of the time it should be fine. However, as I have already said, there is a right and a wrong way to haggle and yelling and demanding a lower rate is certainly not the way to do it.

Having this not been the first time anyone has been angry over the rate, I just kept calm and undaunted and said, "Nope. That is the rate tonight. Sorry."

I was not about to lower the rate just because for a guy that was being an asshole.

Chad grew further displeased with me from my unwillingness to lower the rate for him. He was super important after all. All the while his friend with him just stood still, stoic, and lifeless. To this day I am not convinced the younger of the two men was not a cyborg or just on some great drugs.

Chad demanded, "Give me a lower rate! Now!"

I guess I was not speaking clearly enough the first time. "Sorry I can't. The rate is what it is," I said figuring a second go through would now suffice.

Chad just continued, "That rate is ridiculous. You need to give me a lower rate. Now!"

Maybe third time's a charm. At least I hoped.

"Look I'm sorry sir, but that is our rate tonight," I said once again.

Chad briefly glanced over at his potential cyborg friend and looked back at me. He was continuing to become more upset with me. I could tell from his eyes getting wider and wider. Although I am not convinced Chad was not becoming sexually attracted to me.

He finally spoke and said, "That rate is too high. I work for a company. I should get a rate."

For those of you unaware, hotels often provide negotiated rates for different companies or groups. Some of these discounts are a percentage off the normal rate and some are a flat rate discount. For the record, there is no law stating I must honor any of these rates at any given time (that does include the government per diem). I still did though ask what company he works for.

I inquired, "What company do you work for?"

To which he said, "Johnson Steel. Now give me a lower rate."

I typed in his company into the computer and sure enough I did not have a negotiated rate with any such company.

So, I informed him of this, "Looks like I don't have a rate that company."

Without missing a beat, Chad yelled, "That's ridiculous! You're going to lower the rate! Now!"

At this point I just wanted him to leave. He is just annoying at this point and he is rude and not to mention he has that cyborg standing next to him.

I said to Chad, "Sorry but I don't have a rate with that company. In fact, the rate just went up tonight."

I really wanted them to just leave at this point. This arguing was getting them nowhere. Not to mention Chad was just being rude and annoying. The rate really was not that high and there are plenty of other hotels in town he can try his bullshit haggling at. I was just not having it. Chad however, did not understand that I wanted him to leave and insisted on keeping this argument going.

"Ridiculous! I expect you to cut the rate in half right now! You can't just raise the rate!" Chad said while raising his voice.

I stayed calm and said, "There is no chance whatsoever of me cutting the rate in half for you. Also, I indeed can raise the rate. In fact, it will continue to keep going up the longer you argue. Now we can stay here and argue over it or you can take your business elsewhere until you find something you think is more reasonable. I'd hurry though because my rates just went up another $20."

The argument then continued back and forth of him demanding I lower the rate and me refusing for some time. It was like arguing with a child. And all the while his cyborg friend is standing there silently glaring.

After much time of going back and forth, Chad leaned in real close and said to me, "Listen here fucker, you are going to lower that Goddamn rate right now or else you're gonna be real fucking sorry."

I could not help but be amused by this apparent threat. This conversation went from monotonous and annoying to hilarious at the drop of a hat.

I laughed and then said to Chad and the cyborg, "Dude, you need to get the fuck out of here," while pointing to the door.

One more time Chad yelled, "Lower the damn rate!"

Of course, my immediate response was, "No."

This angered Chad and the younger assumed cyborg a great deal. So much so that they began trying to reach across the desk to grab at me.

I'm not sure what they thought assaulting me, while on camera nonetheless, would get them but it certain will not help their cause. Luckily there was enough space between them and I with the desk in the way that all I really had to do was lean back a bit to stop either of them from being able to grab a hold of me.

"You little shit! I'm gonna kick your ass!" Chad promulgated.

Your body really does have an amazing flight or fight response. My slight dodging of their advancements was my flight response. Running through my head was that I will probably have to get the police involved but until then I want to avoid an actual altercation if possible. But then they kept inching closer, and within those milliseconds, my brain had different thoughts running through it.

Going through my head was the fact that these two guys are threatening me and trying to grab at me now. Not to mention they are both wearing coats, so I have no way of knowing if either of them were at all armed. I need to do something. I have a right to defend myself after all.

Then it hit me. This all within those milliseconds. It really is amazing what your mind does. I recalled that, on several occasions, guests who had stayed had gone hiking in national parks or gone on hunting trips and felt the need to purchase bear mace. Then, being as they could not bring such a thing on a plane, they left it with us at the desk. One of these cans of bear mace happened to be sitting in the drawer next to me… And I really have no other way of defending myself at this point…

I quickly opened the drawer and pulled out the bear mace. I swung it up my finger on the trigger mechanism.

I said almost cheerfully, "This is gonna happen."

I have never seen two guys run so fast in my life. I did not spray any bear mace at all. But you could almost see in that small bit of time as I was swinging the canister up that the gears in their head were going into overtime and the words "Oh shit he's serious" practically appeared in a thought bubble above their heads.

They at least had the common sense to not come back for further arguments. The rest of my night was so unbelievably quiet after that. There always must be some crazy moment every day I suppose.

THIS IS CASH

The golden rule in hospitality or really anything involving customer service is that "the customer is always right." Well anyone who has worked in customer service to any capacity knows what a pile of horse shit that is. Your own stupidity and ignorance will not change facts.

This all leads me to the story of this lady... Who obviously skipped every day at school where there was anything to do with learning about money or counting money. Either that or she has been completely removed from society to the point where she was living in a cave somewhere with Randy Quaid.

This story begins towards the end like a Tarantino movie.

It was a brumal and frigid morning. I was standing at the desk periodically helping guests and in between helping them with their various wants and needs I would observe and make up stories about each of them to pass the time.

I noticed a guest who looked like Ted Turner. What made it especially great is he had a van just like the A-Team had. Watching him it became clear that he was indeed Ted Turner. He had gone insane, bought the A-Team van, and began to embody each of the A-Team characters. Not necessarily in that order though.

During my woolgathering of whom I decided was Ted Turner, a woman walked up to me, and like with most crazy people out there, she did appear to be normal.

This woman comes up to check out of her room. She said to me, "Hi, we are checking out today and I need to come by because I paid cash."

So, at my hotel the cash policy always was that if you pay cash when you check in we would require the full room and tax for your stay as well as an additional $150 security deposit that you would receive back at checkout upon inspection of the room.

So, if you did not damage the room, make any long-distance phone calls, smoke in the room, or manage to cover the walls and floor with large amounts of various bodily fluids (and yes that has happened), then you would get your $150 back.

Basically, it is more hassle than it is worth to do. So, if you want to pay cash, just give us your card at check in and pay cash on your way out.

This woman comes up to me and informs me that she has paid cash for her room. I pull up her room number and see a Mastercard on the room.

I said to her, "Actually ma'am it looks like I have a Mastercard on here for you…" Then thinking that maybe I misheard or misunderstood what she was saying and maybe she wanted to pay cash instead of keeping everything on her card.

I continued, "Were you saying you wanted to pay cash for your room?"

She said, "No I paid cash for my room when we checked in, and I was told there would be an extra charge of $150 that I would get back at check out and I want to make sure that it is taken care of."

I was a bit puzzled. She is saying one thing and I am seeing another. I decided to just politely spell it out for her.

"Well I'm not seeing any cash payment on your reservation ma'am. It looks like I have a Mastercard on file for you here though. So, I am a bit confused. Were you wanting to go ahead and pay cash because that won't be a problem," I said.

Her response left me even more confused. She said, "No that's actually not a real Mastercard. And now I'm worried about extra charges and I need this taken care of."

So apparently her credit card is not real and is from Middle Earth or some universe her and her friends made up for a Dungeons & Dragons campaign that her and her loser friends are putting together.

"Well somehow a Mastercard was swiped at check in and that is what I have on file," I said to her.

She responded, "Yes I gave a Mastercard at check in and there was mention of extra charges and I just want to know what exactly I'm being charged. I just don't understand."

So somehow this card that was not real previously has been birthed into existence. I wonder what would have happened if I asked her if she believes in Santa Claus.

I decided to try a visual aid and show her a copy of her receipt. Thinking to myself that if I show her and point out what exactly her receipt shows that I will exhaust all logic and reason and if she still is incapable of understanding then there is no hope.

I printed out her receipt. I laid it on the desk. Then I began to show her that I had a Mastercard attached to her reservation and the last 4 digits of it. Immediately following I pointed out the price of the room and then the amount of the taxes which brought us to the total which was shown in bold print at the bottom.

She paused and looked at it for a while before asking, "So like this is what I'm going to be charged then?"

Feeling like a broken record I said, "Yes, this is all that we are going to charge you."

There was another moment of pause before she said, "But like what about this extra $150 I was supposed to be charged?"

I was losing all hope if it was not already gone entirely. I was contemplating silently walking away and just driving home leaving her in suspense. It probably would have solved the same amount of problems.

I decided to try again with her. Partly in my absolute last shred of hope that she would get it or that she would be crushed under the weight of the overwhelming power of her own stupidity and die. Secretly I was hoping for the latter of the two.

I pointed out again the price of the room, the taxes, and what this totaled out to. Before she could say anything, I said again that we did not take an extra $150 out because she gave us a Mastercard at check in.

This was followed up by yet another awkward pause. I could see the gears in her head begin to combust. This was all too much logic and reason for her to take all at once. This is why we can't have nice things.

She then said to me, "But that Mastercard isn't a real card. I don't understand. What all are you charging me?"

I have never been an intravenous drug user but right around this time it seemed appropriate to start. Whatever would help me disassociate from this and take the pain away.

So, one more time I pointed out each itemized thing on her receipt. Then proceeded to hand her said receipt thus suggesting that we are done here, and she can leave the desk now.

I thought I was finally free of her fatuous behavior. This was not my morning for anything to work out as I would hope.

Not two minutes later she comes up to the desk while holding her receipt and said to me, "Okay, so I'm going to need a receipt for my stay, so I know what you guys are charging me."

I stared at her like Samuel L. Jackson's character stared at people in the movie "Pulp Fiction." One could say I was staring mothafuckily.

Then I looked outside at my car and looked towards the freeway. I thought to myself, "It would be so easy. I could have my life back."

I finally opened my mouth to tell her, "You are literally holding on to your receipt ma'am."

She looks at her receipt and looks back at me and says, "Really?"

"Yes... I promise that is it," I said.

Finally, she walked away. The clouds had lifted. There is a God.

I managed to go the rest of my shift without dealing with her again by nothing short of a miracle.

My replacement, Calvin, arrived. I pulled him aside to brief him on this woman I spent my morning dealing with.

Not long into it Calvin's eyes lit up and he said to me, "Oh my God! I know what lady you are talking about!"

Intrigued I asked him to go into more detail.

Calvin articulated, "She came in and said she wanted to pay cash. I explained to her the cash policy. She said 'Okay' and held up her card and was ready to swipe. I asked if she was just going to pay cash at checkout then and she said, 'No this is cash!' All I could think to tell her was that no it's a credit card, and she told me that it wasn't a real card and that it was cash. Then we argued back and forth. She truly thinks her credit card is cash. She's a fucking idiot."

He further went on to say, "I actually told her no and that cash was paper money and got cash out of the till and showed her what cash was."

I was feeling a combination of relief that I was not the only one to deal with her, sadness and frustration that my coworker and friend of many years now had to deal with this lady, and sheer bewilderment that anyone ever could not understand the difference between the two.

Although she checked out that day I cannot imagine she made it home. She probably did the opposite of everything her GPS told her to do and then after so many wrong turns she drove herself off a cliff. Oh well I guess.

THAT'S A CRIME

Something is bound to happen any time someone calls in sick. Murphy's Law has shown us this time and time again.

It will not ever have anything to do with whatever illness the person calling in sick has; however, it will always result in you being welcomed into the depths of hell.

This night that I was working when a coworker called in was especially forestalling of any plans I may have had.

Everything worked out, but I was going to have to work 12 hours. I have done it on multiple occasions but sometimes getting a decent amount of sleep just seems so enjoyable.

The night was quieting down. If I had to be there for 12 hours going into the middle of the night, then it was nice to not hear the shrieks of abhorrent children and their asshat parents who wrap their over privileged children in bubble wrap.

All was as good as it could be on such a long shift. I decided to go to the back office and turn on Netflix. Something had to get me through the night after all.

Then the sliding doors parted, and a man walked in to get a room.

This man can only be described as an unfunny, non-descript, balding middle-aged man. His name was Robert. He even looked like a Robert.

He had the greasiest forehead I had ever seen. It was like this guy was sweating Crisco while going through puberty again. This could not have been natural. He probably smears his whole face with lard while dancing and singing in front of his mirror.

Piecing the entire puzzle together, especially being as he walked in right when I was beginning my night of Netflix, I knew this guy was going to somehow end up being a total loser.

He asks about a room and rate as one does when trying to acquire a place to sleep for the night. I told him the price for that night for what he wanted. He agreed and pulled out his credit card and driver's license.

I begin booking his room and he starts to engage me in conversation.

Robert asked me, "Hey, out of curiosity, do you guys have those suites with the jacuzzi tubs in the room?"

I told him, "Unfortunately no, it was an ownership decision for whatever reason."

I was hoping the conversation would end there. Deep down I knew such an aspiration was likely out of the question.

Robert continued as expected. He just shook his head and said, "Well if you ask me that was a dumb decision on their part."

I shook my head in agreement and said to him, "Yeah I'm inclined to agree. It would be great selling point."

I was neutral about the whole situation. I deep down just was hoping he would go away. He smelled like cabbage and I've got shows to watch.

He continued his verbal incursion of my long night, "Exactly that would be great! I guess he just wasn't thinking or something."

Wanting to give a short answer in hopes to end this conversation and send him on his way to be a cabbage smelling failure of a human being somewhere else.

I responded, "Yeah, would be a selling point. Ya know, more money."

Figuring this would put us in a place where any further discussion would just make this conversation redundant, I left it at that.

Robert saw an opening though. He began to educate me, "Actually it's a crime to charge people more for rooms like that."

So apparently it is illegal for a hotel to charge for a room with extra amenities such as a jacuzzi tub. Which I guess means every hotel everywhere is doing something illegal.

I just nodded in amusement. I figured any sort of verbal communication would cause further discussion and I was not wanting to see how far down the rabbit hole of stupidity this man was going to go.

He had more to say though. He inquires, "Hey do you guys authorize peoples' credit cards for incidentals at check in?"

For those of who you may not know, when you stay at a hotel and go to check in, the hotel will authorize your credit card for not just the amount but also a little extra for incidentals. This is completely standard for hotels to do. Basically, we just want to know if you go all Johnny Depp on your room that you will be able to pay for it.

So anyway, I told Robert, "Yes we do." Again, wanting to keep this short and simple especially knowing the luck I have with weird guests.

Robert began to enlighten me once again, "Actually it is illegal for hotels to do that too. In fact, it is illegal for banks to not release those funds after you check out of a hotel too. The hotel's insurance is supposed to cover everything. Not the guest. I mean I know it isn't your fault. You just work here and are just doing your job, but you may want to know."

I stared at him like Samuel L. Jackson's character stared at people in the movie "Pulp Fiction." One could say I was staring mothafuckily.

Just as I was about to tell this guy how it works, I paused. Within milliseconds I had this epiphany of what would happen should I do this.

I would say something along the lines of, "Actually, no. You are wrong. If you as the guest decide to wreck the hotel room, then that is entirely on you. You should and would have to pay for it. It is called taking responsibility for being a total douche. The hotel is not going to use its insurance to cover the cost of you being an asshole."

To which he would probably puff up his chest and wipe some forehead grease through his hair and say something like, "You're wrong! It is illegal for the hotel to do that! It is also illegal for you to disagree with me! You're committing a crime! I'm going to call the police! You're going to jail!"

The argument would continue to get out of control and the police would probably show up but be on my side and it would just make for an even longer night.

I decided against such an action. I really needed to avoid having him speak to me any longer than I had to. Instead I just thought I should just nod and agree with everything he says because while he may continue to talk; agreeing with him will at least get him on his way faster.

So, I did so while mentally picturing myself setting him on fire. I saw no other option.

"Come to think of it," he said, "I've been meaning to actually contact corporate about a lot of this sort of illegal activity. Seriously I know you have no control over this. I just need to get this information out there.

In fact, since I am an elite member of your rewards club, it is actually also illegal for hotels to charge me as much as they do."

Except he was not an elite member of our rewards club. He was at the base level. And the hotel is legally allowed to charge any price we feel like.

I wanted to say, "No! You are not an elite member! You are at the base level! Any idiot with an email can sign up and be exactly where you are! You are entitled to nothing! To fucking nothing! And I can charge you whatever I want! MURICA!" And then proceed to laugh maniacally. Because being a base member does not in any way make you special.

I wanted to say all that but all that came out was, "Oh…"

Finally, Robert decided to get going up to his room. I told him which door he could park by that would take him right to the elevator. He instead goes into a totally different door, so he now must walk all the way down the hall. He was carrying a comforter, a suitcase, a pair of women's cowboy boots, and what looked to be a makeup case. He very well could be a real-life Buffalo Bill. He was a self-proclaimed legal expert and Buffalo Bill.

Robert managed to keep quiet for the remainder of the night. So, either he fell asleep upon entering his room and getting his forehead grease all over the place or was arrested by Jodie Foster while he was dancing around in a woman suit and makeup.

DO YOU KNOW THE LEWISONBURGERS?

A lot of strange people will come out before the sun comes up. It is like they cease to exist during the day but once nightfall happens they suddenly blink back into existence.

It was nearing 5am. I had worked literally every other shift that weekend and Monday. I had enough time after work to go home and sleep for a few hours just to come right back to work.

I had just finished off what felt like my hundredth energy drink. I was itching to get out of there and have some actual days off.

The time was nearing 5am and in walks a man who I would not soon forget.

He was an older man. He was shorter with a round balding head and mustache. It was like meeting The Monopoly guy except with a wispy comb over.

So, this guy walks up to me with a big cheeky grin on his face. He laid his forearm across the desk and leans in slightly.

Cheerfully he said, "Hey! Do you know the Lewisonburgers?"

I said back, "I don't know them sir. Did you need me to call their room for you?"

I figured that "the Lewisonburgers" were guests at my hotel. As I was asking him if he needed me to call them I was also trying to look them up in my in-house guests, but I could not find them or any name even remotely close.

This man, whom we will call Alex, kept his cheeky grin and just said, "Well ya know, they're friends of mine."

This really did not answer any of my internal or external questions.

Still wanting to give this guy the benefit of the doubt I continued, "Okay, well you know sir, I'm actually having trouble locating any guests with that name. You wouldn't happen to know a room number or maybe if they're staying with another group or party that would have put their reservation under a different last name?"

Alex was just remaining in the same posture leaning on the desk with the same grin on his face. He looked like a game show host posing for a picture but had been frozen in time by some evil wizard.

Wanting to break this awkward silence I said, "So... Would their reservation have been made under a different name?"

Once again, he said, "Well they're friends of mine and was wondering if you knew them."

"I don't know them," I said, "Are they guests here? Did you need my help getting a hold of them?"

I was not ready to give up on using logical lines of questioning just yet. I could tell he wanted something and was sure it that it must be something obvious.

Keeping his oversized smile, Alex said to me, "Well they are friends of mine and sometimes they like to stay here when they are in town."

As soon as he said that I looked up the name and found nothing of the sort for past, present, or future reservations. Nothing even that had been cancelled. This only added to my confusion.

All I could think to say at this point was, "Well I'm not seeing any guests here with that last name. You sure they're staying here?"

Alex nodded his head like he at least comprehended what I was asking, "Well you see they're friends of mine, and I wasn't quite sure if they were staying here."

"Well I don't have them here sir," I said.

He paused a quick moment still with the smile of a game show host or a used car salesman and asked, "So you don't know the Lewisonburgers?"

It was about this point I was wondering if he was just wondering if someone else knew these people "the Lewisonburgers." Like somehow these people are the coolest people ever and just knowing them gives you bragging rights.

I said to Alex, "Nope, sure don't know any Lewisonburgers."

Then following up to make sure in case he was asking if they were staying at the hotel, "You don't have a possible room number for them or maybe another name they may be staying under like with a group or something?"

Gleefully Alex said to me, "Nope! Just wondering if you knew them by chance."

Confused I just said, "Nope, sure don't."

Alex turns around and walks towards one of the chairs in the lobby. He then stops at it, turns directly around facing the desk, and saunters back up to the desk with a twinkle in his eye.

Resting his forearm on the desk, leaning in slightly, and smiling he asks once again, "Hey! Do you know the Lewisonburgers?"

I really did not know what to say right at that moment. He literally just asked me that and it turned into a small conversation.

I thought for sure some TV producer was going to come out to tell me that I am on a hidden camera show.

Or maybe I was in the "The Matrix" and they changed something, and I am now having Deja Vu.

I opened my mouth, but nothing came out. Finally, I began to stutter into full speech, "I... Di... Wait... Di... Didn't you literally just ask me that?"

Alex continued, "Well they're friends of mine."

I took a moment to accept that this was indeed actually happening. This man has indeed gone full asshole.

Trying to end this while still being polite I said, "Nope, sure don't know them. And I have no guests under that name either sir."

Alex just kept that same eerie cheeky grin. I had either exited my known reality and entered a horror movie or this man was on drugs. A lot of drugs. And he was not sharing any of his drugs.

He just cheerfully said, "Well I thought I would check."

Alex then turned right around, walked over towards the chair in the lobby, and then turns right back around and saunters back towards the desk again with the same shit-eating grin on his face.

He once again laid his arm down on the desk and cheerfully asked, "Hey! Do you know the Lewisonburgers?"

This was quickly becoming a "Family Guy" joke and I was not having it. While I was not quite at my wits end with him, I still did not want to just tell him off however I really wanted him to leave.

"No sir," I said, "Can't say I know them and as I already said before I don't have anyone in house by that name either."

Alex kept his same smile and continued to lean slightly on the desk, "Oh...," He said. Then just paused.

I did not say anything back. I was not going to break this awkward silence.

Alex again asked, "So you don't know the Lewisonburgers?"

Before answering I channeled my inner Samuel L Jackson and stared mothafuckily at him.

I was trying to keep my cool and not blow up at this guy. The whole time though I was wondering if he was this crazy or he was just a giant troll.

"No sir. I do not know them," I said holding in my enmity.

Alex just keeps smiling, nods, and turns around. He then walks towards the chair in the lobby and does an about-face and proceeded to make his way back to the desk where he sets his arm down, leans in again and cheerfully asks once again, "Hey! Do you know the Lewisonburgers?"

At this point I did not care if he was in some way insane or was just a giant troll. I was going to troll him. Just because he is acting like an asshole.

I looked at him and answered, "No... Do you??!"

Alex just smiled and in a very smug tone of voice said, "Yeah I do. You see they're friends of mine." As though somehow knowing this family whose existence is in question gave him bragging rights.

My jaw dropped, I widened my eyes and exclaimed, "Oh my God!" Playing along like I give a shit about him knowing or not knowing these people.

Alex turned a bit to the side and looked his fingernails and smirked at me, "Yeah I know them. They're friends of mine."

Keeping the same look of amazement and surprise I said, "WOW!"

Alex just continued, "Yeah the Lewisonburgers are friends mine."

To which I said, "Oh my God!"

Right then this flight crew that was staying with us began to make their way out the door to get a ride up to the airport.

Alex looks over at them walking out the door, looks back at me and says, "Must be a flight crew or something." As though this was not super obvious.

Holding my look of amazement, I sharply looked over at the flight crew leaving and then looked back at Alex and exclaimed, "Oh my God!"

He let another moment of pause pass before asking again, "So you don't know the Lewisonburgers?"

This whole time I have kept myself wide-eyed and mouth open. I replied to him, "No... I wish I did though."

Alex just sort of shrugged a bit and said, "Oh okay. Well thanks anyway."

I was more expecting a response of, "Do not pass go. Do not collect $200."

He then sauntered off out of the hotel, and I never saw him again.

I can only imagine he just went from hotel to hotel asking the same damn question to everyone.

At some point he probably pissed off the wrong person who then had a psychotic episode and killed this guy. Here's to hoping at least.

A COP AND HIS GUN

After a certain point, while working in hospitality, where you see so many strange, interesting, and stressful situations that not only do you not find yourself in the least bit surprised but it in fact just adds to the twisted sense of humor that you have developed.

Such a time is the story I am about to tell you:

There my coworkers and I were at the desk just working one afternoon like normal. When suddenly a man comes frantically rushing up to the desk looking like he had just seen a ghost.

This man was wearing a CrossFit t-shirt, jean shorts, and socks with his sandals as if to advertise just how completely stupid he really was. I could feel myself getting dumber just looking at him.

"I need to speak to a manager," he proclaimed.

Henry who was manager on duty at the time spoke up and asked, "Well that would be me right now. What can I do for you?"

"My name is Kevin. I'm in town visiting. I'm a police officer where I live. I just need you to understand that. I was cleaning my gun and apparently, I still had a round in the chamber unbeknownst to me. Well... It went off accidentally and it went through into the room next to mine... I ran over to that room and pounded on the door but got no answer and I am worried someone may have been hurt or killed. I am so sorry! Can we please find out if anyone is in there?" Kevin said as he began to tear up.

Henry's eyes got huge. Trying to maintain composure Henry quickly looked up that room in our property management system said to Kevin, "Okay luckily there was no one checked into that room. However, we should still go look in there to make sure. And I will have to be calling the police because a firearm was discharged."

"Yes, I understand. Of course." Kevin said trying to hold back his inner panic.

They both walked away leaving me curious as to what was happening upstairs, but more so wondering why someone who is obviously has the mental capacity of a stale ham and cheese sandwich can be around firearms much less enforce any laws whatsoever.

Maybe this just comes from having grown up in an open carry state but the first thing I would do after removing the magazine would be to clear the chamber, and I should not have to explain such a thing to someone working in law enforcement. But then again as I had stated this man was indeed a stale ham and cheese sandwich. He must have been single too. Probably killed his last wife.

It was not five minutes after Henry and the sandwich cop left the desk that the local police arrived.

They walked in and I greeted them with a shit eating grin and asked, "Are you guys here for all the fun?!"

The two police officers that had arrived just smiled and kind of chuckled a bit and asked where they are headed to. I cheerfully told them the room number and gave them a thumbs up. Both officers then walked around the corner to the right to where the elevator is.

For the next few minutes I waited with anticipation on what could be happening upstairs.

The police officers came down alone and waived saying, "Have a good day." I was disappointed. I was hoping to see someone go out in cuffs. I know it was not likely unless something further happened past this sandwich of a man accidentally discharging his firearm, but one can always hope for a bit more entertainment.

I had to stop them before they got out the door. I asked them, "So… How did that go?"

The officer leading the investigation just looked at me and said, "You know, I could give him a ticket for discharging his firearm in the city limits and blah blah blah… But you know, that's a lot more paperwork than I care to do today. Besides, he must call his supervisor and whatever his supervisor does to him is going to be a lot worse than anything I can do… He's lucky no one was injured or killed."

A moment after they had left Henry came back to the desk with Kevin the sandwich. Henry had to break the bad news to him that we would have to charge him for the room damages which he understood and agreed to. Not that we would have cared if he didn't understand or agree.

We moved Kevin rooms and put his old room and the room next door where the bullet went into out of order for the next while.

I had to see the damage with my own eyes. Naturally I skipped upstairs to witness the would have been carnage.

So, what had happened with this Kevin guy was he was sitting at the desk up against the wall. His gun discharged at an angle where the bullet went through the pillow on the bed, bounced around in the mattress, went through the head of the mattress, through the headboard, through the wall, into the chair that was pushed up against on the other side in the wall in the room next door, and then finally rattled around in the chair where the bullet eventually just stopped.

Of course, I pulled out my phone and got pictures of the damage to send to all my friends, so they too can see what a dumbass this guy is.

Now I would like to be able to give this guy a shout out. However, I have a feeling in all his stupidity that he accidentally locked himself in his car out front of his house and died of starvation or something equally stupid.

YOUTH HOCKEY TEAMS

There are terrible guests and then there are youth hockey teams. They are the Rosie O'Donnell of the Lesbian X-Games of terrible. Giving the world terrible a new meaning. The kids on these teams are little shit heads and the parents are worse and live vicariously through their little shit heads. Let me tell you a bit about them:

An entire generation of hockey parents threw away the churches and daily services to worship at the altar of their children's greatness. The problem was, the altar turned out to be my hotel hallways at 3am every night, and the congregation was always full.

They had the entitlement unfit for a king.

Part of everyone's job is to be nice to people even when they are being rude. We do our best to deescalate the situation. We try and get the hockey moms and hockey dads to trade in the hockey sticks and pucks for a cup of chill-the-fuck-out. There is however, a 'No Abuse' policy. Eventually we do start getting mean back and eventually will kick someone out sometimes with police present.

When hockey teams were in town it was the one time of year when we ate all the carrots and whipped out our sticks. We did not start out nice and attempt to deescalate the situation before getting mean with them. We instead just start out with both guns blazing. We tried to be nice. We really did. They take kindness for weakness and will try to walk all over you like the pretentious assholes they are.

Youth sports teams always tend to get a bit rowdy. I am not saying anyone who works in a hotel enjoys it one bit...but we do at least expect it. Usually all it takes for them to quiet down is a call to the room, the parents, chaperone, coach, etc.… But with hockey teams it was a different story. The kids were awful, and the parents were even worse.

Each night in which they infested our hallways and bedrooms inadvertently provided hours of resentment-filled entertainment. Much of which does get very repetitive.

I know I am ranting but I just need to vomit on the pages to express my hatred and resentment before getting on with the juicy details.

So here they are. I have compiled some of my more memorable experiences for all of you to enjoy:

Hockey in the Halls

When I was 16, peace and quiet was worth the dirt under my boots. Now, it's 18-year whiskey in Al Capone's Chicago valuable. This next story shows that value and reveals a pet peeve of mine. Something that annoys me to no end. This has really made me learn to value peace and quiet.

These youth hockey groups have this annoying habit of playing hockey in the hallways. At times even until 3 A.M. because to them the perfect time and place to be playing hockey is inside of a building that does not belong to any of them where they can wake people up and potentially cause damage.

I used to want to ask if their parents allow them to do this at home, but I know the answer is yes. Their parents were horrible people and the prime enablers of their children's terrible behavior. I guess on the plus side this gives job security to those individuals who work in corrections.

I still recall my first time dealing with this. I had left the desk to go put an end to these kids playing hockey, raping the hallways with their shrill shrieks and faded potential. During my quest for noiselessness, one of their moms steps out into the hall from behind a door and yells at me, "You can't tell my kids what to do!" I had to smile: it was a declaration of confidence. It was triumphant. It was laced with about nine ounces of whiskey over four hours. It was bold. It was also about to get smacked the fuck down.

My sharp response was, "Actually I can tell your kids what to do. You see, I work here, and this is not allowed."

"That is bullshit," she oozed from two swollen balloons that passed for lips. Lips that probably hadn't touched her husband's Johnson (ironically her last name was also Johnson) in a decade, "We are paying to be here!"

"Well ma'am I've been doing some research and," I drew in close to her now, smelling the liquor on her breath "and, ah, apparently, everyone else also seems to be paying to be here as well, and they don't want to be bothered. Not to mention if one of your children were to cause any damage, you get to pay for it!" I said back to her.

This mom scoffed, raised her arms inquisitively and asked, "Well where exactly are they supposed to be playing hockey then, huh?"

Immediately I responded, "Not here! Maybe try... I don't know... A hockey rink?"

This unleashed a PTO-level of parental self-righteousness. She then lectures me about what great kids they are, and how this is youth hockey, and everyone needs to be supportive because it is better to be part of youth sports and programs than out taking drugs.

Well you know who else had a youth program? Hitler.

The issue of hockey being played in the halls was forever and ongoing issue. It was like Original Sin, or feminists with blue hair: an inescapable, eternal recurrence. I really felt insane telling them again and again to stop and hoping that this would be the time it would work.

One year when they were being especially bad, I got a noise complaint (one of many I received that night) from one of our regulars named Phil.

Let me give you a little back story on Phil. Phil was one of our very regular guests. He owns his own business. He is a super awesome guy. He would always come by and chat with everyone at the desk. One of the nicest guys you could ever meet. I had never seen Phil upset.

Well that night Phil called me at the desk and was livid. He said to me, "Dude. It is fucking late. I have to wake my ass up early in the morning and meet with some potential big money clients and I cannot deal with these kids playing hockey in the halls."

I apologized and said, "This is an ongoing problem. I am doing my best to put an end to it. I will head right up there."

Phil then asked, "Can I just tell them I'm the owner of the hotel and they need to be quiet before I kick them out."

"You sure can Phil!" I said. This sounded like a great idea.

So, Phil went out in the hallway and yelled at these kids and inevitably at their parents.

I suddenly get a call from some hockey parents asking me if this guy yelling at them to be quiet was indeed the owner. Of course, I backed him and said he was and that they better listen to him.

Everyone was quiet after that for the rest of the night. The apparent threat was not strong enough to force them to stop for the rest of that weekend much less forever.

<u>Mother of the Year Award</u>

This was one of my first experiences with the sub-humanoid group we call youth hockey teams.

I cannot stress enough that as bad as these kids got... The parents were even worse. This is a prime example of one of those cases.

The check in process alone was a nightmare.

Before we even had anyone checked in, we had to deal with the absurdity levels being cranked up to 11.

These people drink a lot. I mean A LOT. I really do not think I can stress that enough. Their veins are waterpark slides for whiskey.

This team had shown up early in the afternoon. As they always did they made their presence known with various loud noises and children hitting various objects with their hockey sticks which I suppose was to test the durability in case they wanted to break something later. Leaving scuff marks on the furniture and walls could not have been their only objective.

After the initial chaos, the parents stuffed some of their kids into rooms to watch television and some of them they took to the pool area to serve as the acting babysitter while the parents got shitfaced.

The time was now roughly 7 P.M. I looked up and I see a woman roughly in her late 30's. She was wearing a sort of grey-blue polo shirt, khaki capris, no shoes, and she of course had the "I need to speak to your manager" haircut.

I see this woman stumbling down the hallway towards the desk drunk, with the bottle of liquor in hand, and in her barely intelligible voice utters the words, "Have you seen my daughter?"

Allow me to just summarize the scene here. It is maybe 7 P.M. and this woman is already sloshed. She is now stumbling around bottle in hand. And then the real kicker is she has now misplaced a 4-year-old child.

If I did not already before, I now officially hate this woman. However, I am now dealing with a lost child. So now I must make this lost child's safety my primary concern because obviously this mother has so much disregard that she would allow total strangers to fill in where needed.

So, we began searching the hallways. Going up and down the stairs and riding the elevators. We had someone go outside and circle the parking lots. We even went as far as to start calling teammates rooms and asking them if they had seen her, but no one had.

We decided it was best to call the police. There was now drunk mother and a missing 4-year-old child.

Beer Run

We had two teams in at this time. They were a typical hockey bunch. A loud, obnoxious group who, like a wild predator with a taste for blood, they could not get enough destruction.

This story begins where it ends; with a hockey dad walking up to me late one evening towards the end of this go around with teams.

We had already dealt with several days of typical hockey team shenanigans. Then late one evening, the night before the last game, one of their dads approached me at the desk.

We had two teams staying. These two different teams were going head to head and now staying in the same hotel.

He said, "Well it looks like the other team won't be playing us tomorrow after all."

To which I responded, "Oh that's a bummer." My only reason for responding was honestly just to give him some thought of validation is commenting at all in hopes he would just leave because I really did not care to talk to him.

The hockey dad continued, "Yeah they ran into a little bit of legal trouble and yeah, they won't be playing. They all went home and had to forfeit the game tomorrow."

This now piqued my interest a bit. The idea of hockey teams having any sort of misfortune especially when it leads to them forfeiting a game and especially when the cause may be legal problems... I'm not going to lie, it made me smile.

I said to this hockey dad, "Please continue. I'm intrigued."

That is when he told me the tale of their misfortune.

You see many of these kids' parents thought it would be okay to allow them to drink alcoholic beverages. Somewhere between these parents wanting to be cool, living vicariously through their children, and being raging alcoholics themselves they did not see what could possibly go wrong providing alcohol to a bunch of rowdy 13-year olds.

After they consumed a large amount, these kids decided they wanted to drive down to a convenient store and steal another case of beer. Being as they were intoxicated and not old enough to drive, such a thing would most certainly lead to jail time. How could this decision get any worse?

Well to make matters worse, they all decided to try to steal a car.

So, they find a car and managed to get inside of it. Naturally, the next step was to try to get it hotwired, so this vehicle would start. During this time, they were having issues and while one person was in the vehicle the rest of these kids were rocking the car trying to get it to start because drunk logic.

Instead of starting the car ended up gaining just enough forward momentum to rock forward and run the bumper into a light pole.

During all this the owners of the vehicle had noticed this obvious attempt at grand theft auto and called the police.

Once the police showed up all the parents were then brought into the picture and the owners of the vehicle came down as well. Meanwhile the hockey dad informing me of what was going on was just a fly in the conversation.

In short, the deal that was struck was that they would all pack up right then and go back home and call in and forfeit the game.

I was very much pleased to learn of their misfortune. The only downside is that none of them went to jail. If I were the owner of that vehicle I would have pressed charges. But I guess them having to forfeit, go home, and be kicked out of their hockey league is still good.

<u>Xbox</u>

Noise complaints happen. In fact, they happen often. When hockey teams are around, this becomes a constant issue. As if we did not already have enough reason to hate them.

There was one night that was especially bad for noise complaints. Especially from one group of teenagers.

This group of teenagers were all gathered in room 126. They congregated like maggots on a fresh wound to play Xbox all together, but I don't want to insult maggots.

Among normal everyday guests this would not be an issue at all. In fact, many people bring game consoles of different sorts and there was no issue whatsoever.

But these were not normal guests. These were hockey families. These are people who's only redeeming quality is that they eventually leave.

The parents were sitting out in the breakfast area drinking heavily. I'm not joking about it being heavy drinking. There was a small group of parents and enough alcohol to kill a herd of elephants.

While the parents got drunker than a college frat party, they left their teenage kids all piled into one room just down the hall to play Xbox, the babysitter that never talks back.

As if the drunk parents were not loud and obnoxious enough, I could hear their kids all the way down the hall yelling and screaming at whatever was going on that seemed to amuse them.

It was not just me that heard them. I was getting noise complaints for their room from several floors up.

I called the room time and time again.

At first, I would call and say, "Hey! I'm getting some noise complaints. I need you guys to keep it down for me."

Their response was a very typical, "Uh okay. Sorry."

There really are only so many times I can ask politely to normal people much less this group of sub-humanoids. My patience was being tested and it would not find itself with a passing score. I had to accept the inevitability that my anger would indeed erupt.

My calls to the room quickly went from, "Hey! I'm getting some noise complaints. I need you guys to keep it down for me" to, "I am getting calls from literally everyone except your drunk ass parents. If you guys cannot keep it down there will be consequences." Which was followed up by me going to speak to their drunk ass parents to tell them that the whole lot of them need to be quiet and behave like semi-decent people who have at least a small grasp of functioning in society.

As was their custom, they did not listen. In fact, they got louder.

I was not having this anymore. I marched out to the breakfast area and angrily lectured the parents about their obvious drinking problem and disturbing everyone while letting their kids be assholes. Their apathy only fueled my anger more.

Then I made my way to the room this group of teenage anthropoids were congealing.

I said to them, "Look. This is your last chance. Keep the noise levels down to a minimum or that Xbox is going to become mine."

The kid who answered the door looked a bit concerned and said, "Uh okay." And then shut the door again.

I made my way back to the desk fully aware that this would not be the last I would hear from them.

As expected within five minutes I am hearing yelling coming from that room down the hall, and then the noise complaints start to roll in.

I was about to go down to the room and rip out their Xbox. I really was. But then in a moment I thought about the noise that would follow and then having to yell at their angry parents and that I would ultimately have to give it back.

So, in the blink of an eye I had a better idea.

I ran down the hall in the opposite direction towards the electrical closet. I found the breaker to their room and just shut off the power.

Of course, not long after I had made my return to the desk I get a phone call. I answered to see on the caller ID that it was that very room calling.

Gleefully I answer, "Guest services how may I help you?"

The voice on the other end said to me, "Uhhh… The power in room went out."

I pushed the phone closer to my mouth and with a deeper, dark, supervillain voice, barely a whisper, responded with, "Don't fuck with the Jedi master." Then just hung up the phone.

A waited a few and then went and turned the power back on to their room. I did not hear another peep out of those kids. The parents were a different story but eventually I got them to take their heavily intoxicated selves up to their rooms. I wasn't lucky enough to have any of them die of alcohol poisoning though. I guess none of us were that lucky that night.

I won that battle though. Jedi Mind Tricks always prevail.

Finally, I just want to speak directly to all the hockey families out there. This is partially directed towards the kids but more directed towards the parents. This is a message for all of you.

No one likes you. Just stop being such pathetic excuses for human beings. I would think that such a task would not be so incredibly difficult, but you have all shown me otherwise.

So, put the bottle down and go to a 12 steps group and then get these little chthonic entities created from accidental ejaculations that you call your children under control.

WHINING WON'T GET YOU INTO THE POOL

Our next tale of misadventure takes us to another night of working night audit...

Before we dive into this story it is important that I explain something right off the bat. It has to do with the procedure for when I must leave the desk for whatever reason while working overnight, which is often.

I am sure that every hotel has their own procedure for this. I cannot imagine they are too incredibly dissimilar, but I could very well be wrong.

We had this sign that we would put up at the desk that read as follows:

> I am currently away from the desk assisting another guest or performing other duties that require me to be away. Please use the phone labeled **House Phone** on the table in the front of the fireplace to contact me. I apologize for the inconvenience, and I appreciate your patience and understanding in the matter!

So, the "House Phone" was programmed to when you pick it up it immediately calls the front desk and only the front desk. This way when I had to leave I could hit a button on the desk phone and all incoming calls would be forwarded to the portable phone we had that I would take with me. Or if I am just sitting in the back office watching Netflix I would not forward it but come out as soon as the phone rings.

I do understand that next to no guests are going to understand that this is what is going on. However, if you are staying at a hotel and you walk up to the desk to find no one there but there is a sign clearly sitting on the desk in plain sight... the logical thing to do in this case is to read it because it may have information about how to get someone's attention.

It is as amazing as it is sad, but majority of people lack this sort of logic to piece this together.

Of the people who will not read the sign, a greater majority will at least say "hello" in an inquisitive tone, but there still remains those who wish to cough or clack their keys on the desk or say "ding ding ding" or do something else of equal or greater annoyance to me.

Then there is that remaining small percent that take their idiocy to new heights. Such a person is the man of whom this story centers around.

So, there I was... at work as usual. I had quickly gotten most of my work done for the night, so I could kick back, and binge watch shows on Netflix uninterrupted.

I was just sitting there minding my own business when suddenly I hear a very confused voice out front say, "Uhhhh... Hello???".

I stand up and walk out of the back office and to the front desk. I see this guy in his early to mid-20's wearing a grey shirt and basketball shorts.

This man's name was Roy, and about the only thing he seemed to be capable of was whining.

I say, "Hi, how can I help you?"

He extended his arm and began waving a $5-dollar bill at me and said, "I uh like uh... Need like change."

I nodded my head and said, "Well don't we all." Then I took the $5 bill from his hand and gave him 5 $1 bills in exchange.

Roy gives me a very confused almost disgusted look and walks away towards the vending machines. I went back to the back office to continue watching Netflix for a bit.

About 15 minutes later I hear that same whining coming from the desk. My sign was clearly on display as it had been the time before as well.

"Hello??!" Roy lamented.

Once again, I walk out there and pull the sign off the desk that was sitting right on front of him.

I noticed he was wearing a green shirt this time. It did not seem to be anything of any real importance no I brushed that off.

"Um so like, I'm gonna need a key." He said.

Guests needing keys to their room due to having lost it or locked themselves out of their room is a daily thing. It really is not any big deal whatsoever.

Not thinking anything of it I asked for his room number and last name as is the standard security procedure.

Roy cocked his head to the side and opened his mouth in confusion. I really did not understand what was so confusing about this line of questioning. In fact, why he was confused by anything I said that night will remain a mystery.

He said, "No. I have a key to my room. I don't exactly need that."

Now I suddenly was feeling confused. If he does not need a key to his room... What exactly does he need?

I just had to ask, "So... Why are you asking for a room key if you don't need one?"

Slightly annoyed Roy said, "Because I need a key to room 204. Last name is Jones."

I paused for a moment and gave him my own look of confusion before asking, "So, you want a key to a room that you aren't staying in? Sorry that's just not going to happen."

Roy's jaw dropped, and he flinched with bewilderment, "What? Why? I need a key to that room!"

I was not swayed by his continuous whining or lack of real argument. I responded, "No... You're not staying in there... So as far as I am concerned you don't need to be in there."

Roy then pulls out his wallet and takes out his license. He handed it to me and said, "Look! They're my family!"

I glanced down at his driver's license and noticed that he had a completely different last name than the people staying in room 204. This only hurt his chances of me giving him a room key which at this point was none whatsoever.

I pointed out, "So I see you have a completely different last name. This is only hurting your chances."

He then throws his arms in the air and stomps his foot repeatedly while letting out a moaning noise like an unruly child. I just stared blankly.

He said, "But like, they're my family!"

To which my response was, "And I don't know that."

Roy pulls out his phone and waives it around and said, "Well she was like talking to me on messenger and telling me to come up! She's like giving me permission."

"Congratulations. I'm very happy for you. If that is the case, why don't you go upstairs and just knock on the door." I said while remaining unmoved.

Roy gave me this almost disgusted look and yelled, "You're an asshole!"

Still remaining stoic I said, "I know. I hate myself too."

Roy stomps off and goes towards the elevator. I went back to watching Netflix and waiting for my shift to be over.

Maybe 10 minutes later I hear an all too familiar man's voice whining at the desk, "Hello???"

Reluctantly I walk out front and say, "How can I help you?" As I took down the sign that was right in front of him again.

I notice this time he was wearing a sleeveless grey shirt this time. I really was beginning to wonder why he needed to change his shirt so often. At the same time though I did not want to ask. Not because I figured he was doing anything creepy or gross but because I really did not want to speak to him any longer if possible.

Roy throws a $20 bill on the desk and said, "So like I need change for the vending machine."

I took the $20 bill and said, "Yeah it comes in handy." Then I proceeded to give him change.

Roy continued to look more and more perplexed. He paused and gave me such a look before walking away towards the vending machine.

I once again went back to watching some Netflix. I was really hoping he was done but I also knew at the same time that this was not likely.

Roughly 30 minutes went by and I heard nothing. Not a peep from anyone. I did notice it was about time for me to deliver folios though. I double checked to make sure my sign was up and set the phone to the portable one before beginning my rounds.

I was finishing up and coming down the stairs I hear, once again, a man whining at the desk.

"Hello?!!! Hello?!!! HELLO?!!!" I heard being repeatedly yelled.

As I got closer I saw him standing at the desk, in front of the sign, again. Just yelling and whining repeatedly again and again.

I quietly walk around to the desk. I walk up and very calmly said, "Yes?"

Roy was holding his arm up with his key card in hand and slightly towards me. All the while he was making this unintelligible whining noise like a toddler who wants attention from their mom.

I just said to him, "I don't know what you're saying."

Roy just kept waving his hand around in the air holding his key card making the same sort of toddler whining noises.

I put my hands on my hips and cocked my head to the side like a parent scolding their child and then said to him, "Use your words."

Roy lowered his hand and gave me a disgusted look before saying, "Uh… Why exactly is my key letting me into my room but not into the pool?"

"Well the pool is closed right now being as it's almost 3 in the morning." I said.

I omitted the part about the lock on the pool door having a timer on it as well and how that all works because I figured this would be beyond his intellectual capacity.

Roy did become a bit angered by my reasons for him not being able to access the pool. He said, "But, I like, wanna go in the pool!"

"Well as I said before, the pool is closed right now. It does though open at 6am. When it hits 6 in the morning feel free to go on in there." I said almost apathetically.

Roy's voice got a little louder as he said, "But I wanna go swimming! Why won't you let me in?!"

Staying perfectly calm and unreactive I responded with, "Because the pool is closed."

Roy still did not get why I was using logic. He said, "So what? You're like just not going to let me use the pool? I wanna go swimming!"

Roy became animated and started to stomp his foot and move his arms around like he was beginning to throw a tantrum. This of course only strengthened my resolve.

"The pool is closed. It will be open at 6 o'clock. You can use it then all you want," I said.

Roy just made a moaning noise and stomped off towards the elevators. Hopefully to finally leave me be for the rest of the night.

I went back to watching Netflix as before. Not long after I heard someone walking around so I just got up figuring it was Roy once again.

I was correct that it was indeed Roy. Although, he did not stop by the desk. He walked around a bit and then stopped at the vending machine. He was wearing a white shirt this time. He stared at the vending machine for quite some time. I suppose you never want to be too hasty when making big important decisions.

Something just came over me. I really needed to have some closure with this guy. Something that would end this while leaving me completely victorious.

I then had an epiphany… I knew what I had to do.

I grabbed the master set of keys that are kept at the desk. I made my way out from behind the desk and began to walk down the hall. I slowed down a bit to make sure to get Ron's attention. I made eye contact with him and smiled slightly. Then I kept walking until I got down to the pool. Ron never stopped watching me the whole time.

Once at the pool room door I started to insert the key into the slot but stopped before sliding it in the lock. I then turned my head around and gave Ron a big giant smile as I unlocked the pool for myself. The look on his face was an amalgamation of anger, confusion, horror, and disgust. That look was truly priceless. I went inside the pool area where I would sit and play on my phone for a good 20 minutes.

THE MOM WHO
HEARS VOICES

So, there I was... Working night audit as I had done many times before, and just when I had thought that I had seen everything at my job... That fateful night happened.

I started off my night as usual. Which, during night audit, involves getting as much done right away as possible so you have more time to screw around by watching Netflix and looking up offensive memes to add to your collection.

Basically, the harder you work at the beginning allows for ample fucking around time after. It is an investment and like any good investment you get a return on your investment. In this case having time to dick around and enjoy not dealing with assholes and psychos all day.

I was standing at the desk diligently working so I could get to go in the back, sit down, and binge watch Netflix. Then a man walked up to me. Because of the following events that transpired I will not ever forget this man, and now I have the pleasure of sharing this story with all of you.

This man walks up to me. He was roughly my height, long brown hair pulled back in a ponytail, brown eyes, darker complexion, and wearing a plaid button up shirt and jeans. He was somewhat soft spoken, and for our purposes today we will call him Jerry.

Jerry walks up to me and asks if I can give him change for the vending machines. So far nothing out of the ordinary. This is an everyday request I get.

I see him go around the corner to the vending machines and gets himself a soda and some M&M's. Jerry comes back up to me at the desk just to talk with me.

There was nothing abnormal about our conversation at that point either. Just mostly small talk. He asked how my night was going and we talked a bit about work and family and what not. Jerry told me he was having a bit of a rough day that was turning into a bit of a rough night, so I may end up seeing him here and there throughout the night.

I do not think that either of us were prepared for just how bat shit crazy that night was about to get.

For the next hour or so I would see Jerry on and off wandering the halls or going outside or whatever. Then suddenly, he wasn't coming by anymore.

Then it all happened. I was just sitting in the back watching some Netflix and minding my own business when I was summoned to the desk…

Jerry was standing there looking tired and frustrated. Even with his obvious stress he still managed to maintain composure and stay somewhat soft spoken. He said to me, "Hey man, I'm really sorry to bother you again tonight."

"That's all right," I said.

He continued, "Hey so my wife went out to our van… This may sound strange but unless I personally say to you that it is okay… I really don't want her coming back up to our room."

Part of me really did not care and did not want to pry, but a bigger part of me had some general concern for everyone's wellbeing and was rather curious. I asked him if everything was okay.

Jerry took a breath and said to me, "Well I just really don't want her up in our room right now. She is saying all sorts of weird, crazy, off the wall shit that makes no sense at all and she is freaking out my kids and me. I really don't know what to do right now…" It almost looked as if he was holding back tears as he then said, "Can you get me the non-emergency number to the police? I really don't know what else to do here and I need someone to come talk to her. I really think she has lost her fucking mind."

I gave him the number to police dispatch and he said he will be back shortly and left.

So now I am on the lookout for a tin foil hat wearing soccer mom. My night just got very interesting, and I am so excited.

Not even two minutes after Jerry had walked away from the desk I get a call from a room. Another guest was woken up by a van's car alarm going on off in the back part of the parking lot. Due to the circumstances and the timing of things I assumed it was Jerry's van. However, I still had to go check it out and hope that I would see a crazy woman jumping on top of it screaming about how the end is nigh.

I did not see that though. Just a van whose alarm going off. You can imagine my disappointment when I didn't see such a thing. When I came back inside I caught Jerry getting off the elevator. I asked if it was his van. He said it was and turned off the alarm with his key fob.

We walked back up the desk where he waited for the police to arrive. He was traveling with his wife and kids and his parents. To be safe he took his kids to their grandparents' room. Eventually the police showed up and he walked them out back.

I gave them a moment then I tried to sneak by the back door, so I could look out the window and watch this shit unfold. I saw Jerry standing with the two police officers and his wife standing there wrapped in a blanket talking to them.

I decided to wait and do the next best thing to watching this shit show which was binge watching some random series on Netflix.

Just as soon as I was getting back into my show Jerry came back up to the desk.

He said to me, "Hey man, sorry for all this commotion tonight. It turns out she set the car alarm off. When I asked her how she did that from the inside she said, 'Oh that was easy. I was kicking the dash to try to get the voices that were coming from the dash panel to shut up.' So, because she admitted in front of the officers that she was hearing voices that weren't there... They're taking her to the hospital for a medical evaluation. Basically, just told her they can do this the easy way or the hard way. She agreed to go without a fight thankfully."

This lady is out of her fucking mind. I to this day wonder what the voices coming from the dashboard were saying to her. Oh, the joys of working overnight. I get to deal with the especially crazy shit.

Jerry decided to further open up to me about all the happenings of his little trip and the mishaps before.

Jerry would go onto say, "Man... This all got started like five days ago. I was just coming home on my lunch break and see her being wrestled on the ground by police officers, my goddamn window is broken, all my neighbors were out there watching this. It was the neighbors next door that called the police... She was screaming about how I was in the backyard fucking some other woman on the trampoline and I had locked her out of the house."

"Wow... Do you even have a trampoline?" I asked.

I guess he does have one. I was just standing across from him listening to all this trying to picture it without laughing.

"I knew shit was really about to hit the fan when we were driving down," He said.

Of course, I had to know this story.

He went on to say, "I was driving down here in our van and everything was totally fine at first, but then the crazy just came out again. She, out of nowhere, grabbed the steering wheel and yelled saying 'Pull this mother fucking car over right now or I'm going to kill us all!' So naturally I pulled the van over and she gets out and just starts running up the highway. Some people stop for her and gave her a ride. I was trying to get her to calm down and come back with me, but she just kept freaking out and told these people that she didn't know who I was and needed a ride into town. We were like 50 miles outside of town. They gave her a ride and when I get to town I'm trying to track her down. Finally get a call from her saying she is at the Salvation Army and I need to come pick her up. Then tonight with all this shit…"

So, I am trying to imagine this guy during this incident. Here he is in his soccer mom minivan driving down the highway with his 2.5 children. You know, his son, his daughter, and a torso or a pair of legs severed at the navel or something. When suddenly, as if living this "Leave it to Beaver" suburban life isn't a nightmare enough, your wife then actively threatens to kill of you just out of fucking nowhere.

I was not sure if I needed to just continue to listen to him and let him vent or crack open the phonebook to find a good divorce lawyer. I am sure he could make one quite wealthy with this sort of case.

Jerry went off to get something from his car and then back up to their room to try to sleep. The next morning, they checked out and I never saw them again. I can only assume he just "forgot" to go pick up his wife from the psych ward at the hospital. I know I would!

THE MAN WITH ONE HAND

Hotel regulars always made my job so simple and so easy. They show up and there really is no awkwardness or worrying about first impressions with being the face of the hotel. When they come by it's a bit of chit chat but for the most part just straight business. They always know the drill.

There are some regulars though that show up occasionally who are not actually guests. This story is about such an individual. He is a guy named Brad. And he is known as the man with one hand.

Brad is on the shorter side with a smaller build. He was middle aged I would say in his mid-50's, and of course… He was missing his right hand.

Brad was one of the city's homeless. Overall, even with his obvious case of schizophrenia, he was a very friendly individual throughout his interactions with the staff at my hotel.

Many of people upon hearing that he was both homeless and schizophrenic felt the need to warn me that I should be careful around him. I always thought this was a bit asinine. I mean what is he going to do nub me to death? Besides, should he ever snap and go ape shit one day I am still safe because I was always nice to him. I would be spared.

Brad would come in at various times of day or night usually wearing a hoodie and jeans. There appeared to be no real pattern to his timing. However, when he did stop by he would swing by the desk, ask if he can grab a cup of coffee, grab his coffee, say thank you, and leave. Sometimes he would stop by and chat a bit. It wasn't too often that he would stop to converse but when he would it was always entertaining to hear what his crazy mind would come up with.

I can recall various times when he would, very briefly, tell me his latest conspiracy theory about dinosaurs still being alive and pulling the strings of government or how Frankie Muniz from "Malcolm in the Middle" was an alien super human like any of us didn't already know that. One of my more favorite times being when he told me that he is undercover with the FBI trying to catch a cannibal in town.

Most of the time his antics were brief and, on his way, out the door… But now and then he would have to stop and talk to us for a bit. It was in these times that everyone at the desk was provided with much needed merriment.

Over time we seemed to become his favorite people and the hotel became his favorite hangout. So just imagine a shorter, frail, homeless man in his 50's, with one hand partying in a hotel lobby like a rapper in some high-end nightclub.

Brad didn't do anything like that but it's quite the visual and I like to imagine it whenever I would see him sitting around that this is what was going on in his mind. I really need to get a life.

Somewhere along the way, Brad got a caseworker to help him claim disability, hopefully find a job, a place to live, etc. I don't think he was ever able to get a lead on a job. I was holding out for him to place a hook where his missing hand would be and fight Peter Pan and the lost boys with his team of pirates. This not happening either was just one more disappointment I was left with at work.

So shortly after he started to get help from this caregiver, Brad decides we are awesome and he wants to stay at the hotel a few nights. This stay of his would open the floodgates to more and more of his stories and hallucinations he wished to share with us.

Brad checks in and for the first bit he was very quiet and only came by to see everyone when he was grabbing coffee. After a while though some friend of his came by to stay with him. This guy that was staying with him was a real person not just a character who lives in Brad's head. I am not sure any of us ever found out this friend's name. I'm still hopeful that it is something cool like Hernandez, but his name is probably something lame and boring like Tom.

After a couple of days of having a party in their room with Count Chocula and H.R. Puff n Stuff or whoever it is that crazy homeless people hang out with; I came into work to find out that Brad got upset at with his friend and leaves the room for a while. I was told that Brad will probably be calling every so often like he had been to voice his vexation.

I had seen Brad's friend, Hernandez or Tom or whatever his name is, walking about and going outside to smoke several times throughout my shift. Then in the latter half of my evening shift I finally received a phone call from Brad.

Brad said to me, "Hey it's me Brad. As you may be aware, I have rented out the room 103. So, I let my friend come stay with me. But I don't want him there no more. I'm not there right now but he is, and I want him gone."

"Oh okay" I said, "I'll just tell him he needs to leave."

Brad continued the conversation, "Oh no. You don't understand. I want him gone. I'm not comfortable with him. He freaks me out. I need him out of there before I come back."

I said, "Yeah man, I understand. I will tell him he needs to leave. It's your name and card on the room. If you don't want him there he doesn't need to be there."

To me this was open and shut. If Brad doesn't want this guy in his room, then I will ask him to leave. I recall thinking that this guy may not want to go quietly, but I have a morbid sense of humor and enjoy watching police drag unruly guests out of my lobby.

Brad continued, "Oh no you don't understand. I'm not comfortable with him and I don't want him in my room anymore. He was saying something to me about how he killed his wife with an axe. I don't want him there. I already called the police and they are going to come take him out of there."

Brad then just hung up. I was not entirely sure if this guy an axe murderer or if Brad just had taken off his foil hat for a moment.

The police finally show up. I directed them to the room and asked if I can watch this guy get tazed. The officer didn't really give me much of a response. He just kind of smirked and let out a chuckle.

Moments later the officers that had arrived on the scene were quietly walking this guy out of the hotel in an incredibly anticlimactic way without a fight. I was really hoping that Hernandez or Tom or whatever the hell is name is would whip out his sweet Kung Fu skills that would ultimately get him tazed but not before an epic battle. Sometimes there is just no winning for me.

Brad called back to make sure that this other guy was gone before he returned the hotel. Eventually he came back, and the remainder of his stay was quiet.

This was not the last we would see of Brad. He went back to his normal routine of showing up every so often to grab a cup of coffee. Although it seemed like from his stay on that he was more likely to let out his inner crazy person to us.

Brad would not share the fantasy world that was his perceived reality with us every time he would come by but when he did it was awesome.

One example being, there was one fateful night where Brad came by to get coffee in the middle of the night. I was fairly focused in on trying to get the rest of my real actual work done so I could get back what was important being Netflix.

Brad walks up to the desk with his coffee. He said to me, "I'm going to need some phone numbers."

"Okay…" I said feeling intrigued and wondering where he was going with this.

As serious as can be and with much conviction Brad said to me, "I need the phone numbers to the United States Marine Corps and the Pentagon."

As quick as I could I hopped on Google to look up these phone numbers for him. I really had to see where he was going with this.

I quickly wrote down the numbers I had found which were the number to the Marine recruiter in town and the 800 number to the Pentagon. I slid the piece of paper with the phone numbers across the desk to him with a shit eating grin on my face. I just could not wait for him to start dialing phone numbers, so I could see the black sedans pull up under the awning within a couple of minutes. I continued to run with this in my imagination.

I could just see in my head him flipping shit and thinking the reptilian space aliens posing as government officials headed up by Tony Danza. This of course is all while he runs outside for the good of the planet.

Brad takes the piece of paper I handed to him and said, "Thank you. I need to contact all of them. There are a lot of evil people at the university!" And then just storms off out the door. I do not know where he was off to, but I bet it was awesome.

A week or two went by and I was there for another graveyard shift where he made his presence known. He walked in wearing his usual jeans and a green hoodie with the words "GOT 420?" written on it in permanent marker.

He went over and got himself a cup of coffee and told me to have a great night and walked out the door. Moments later I saw him sitting outside speaking with two police officers. They were all out there for some time until the two officers just kind of left. This struck me as odd and made me very curious what they were talking about. Being as Brad left that day looking a bit down I am guessing that the officers didn't have any marijuana either.

Well the next night rolls around and in walks Brad to get some coffee again. After he dispenses some coffee and picks up with cup with his one hand and his nub he walked over to me and set it down on the desk for a moment.

Brad then spoke his first words to me that night which were, "You know I'd love to stay and chat with you but I gotta get going. I'm working with the police and the FBI to stop a cannibal that is running around town."

My immediate response was, "Wow man! That is some heavy shit to deal with! Hope you guys catch the fucker!"

He enthusiastically yelled while walking out the door, "We are gonna bring the bastard down!"

Part of me is sure that this is just another delusion of his, but at the same time I could not help but wonder if by some odd chance he somehow came across a cannibal serial killer and was giving the police helpful info into catching this guy.

Brad seemingly disappeared for a while. There just no sight of him for a little while. I was beginning to wonder if maybe he found some other hotel that lets him get free coffee. Maybe he is helping Jeff Goldblum and Will Smith save the world from aliens. Or maybe he is trying to catch the Zodiac Killer. I just noticed it had been a bit since anyone had seen him and it made me wonder.

Well as luck would have it Brad decides to stop by one afternoon. My coworker, Mike, was working the desk when this event transpired.

Mike was speaking to a guest when Brad walks in. Brad goes over to a table, pulls out a piece of paper and a pen, and quickly writes something down. All the while Mike was still with the guest.

Brad starts to walk forward towards the desk. He stands there quietly at first waiting his turn to speak with Mike. Naturally though one can only wait so long before one grows impatient.

Brad waited a whole 20 seconds. It may as well have been an eternity for him. Each of those 20 seconds he grew more and more anxious. Eventually he could not take it anymore and crumpled up his piece of paper that was in his hand and threw it at Mike right before storming out the door.

After wrapping up with the guest Mike was speaking to, he opened the crumpled-up piece of paper. Much to his surprise all it said on there was "Terry Gunderson is traveling to Fairbanks Alaska to kidnap 4 kids."

While it is more likely that Brad was having another delusion or hallucination and trying to warn us of a horrible crime that is about to be committed... I choose to believe that his friend Terry Gunderson, while real or imaginary, was planning on traveling to Fairbanks, Alaska to kidnap four children and Brad just wanted to come by and brag about it.

Well, all good things must come to an end I suppose.

I came into work like any other day. I was wearing my button up shirt and slacks and no tie because I had pretty much given up already that day.

There is a grocery store that is just a hop, skip, and a jump away from the hotel... I come to work to learn that Brad, in all his schizophrenic glory, was arrested. And that was basically the last we heard from him.

A CUP FULL OF NOTHING

Have you ever witnessed something that made you wonder if you were seeing exactly what you were seeing?

Mark Twain once said, *"I've lived through some terrible things in my life, some of which actually happened."*

Which is extremely applicable as I kept replaying the events that occurred again and again because I was not sure if what I witnessed had actually taken place.

Well allow me to tell you about such an occurrence I had.

I came in to work for a night audit shift, and was greeted by my coworker Calvin.

Calvin said to me, "Okay, so the lady in room 301 is fucking crazy."

Being as this was the beginning of my night, I found myself intrigued. So I asked Calvin to elaborate.

Calvin went on, "Okay so I got here like right at 3 today. Then right after I got to the desk she came to check in. First thing she asks for is a place she can get food and alcohol. So I gave her a couple suggestions. Then I asked for her credit card and photo ID. That is when she started to argue about giving me her ID. She got all flustered and said, 'Why? Why do I need to show you my ID?' So I tried explaining that it was hotel policy and that identity theft is a thing. She just kept arguing and saying she just doesn't understand and just kept arguing. No matter how much logic and reason I used."

"Well she sounds like a real winner," I said.

"Well that is when it got really weird," Calvin said, "She checks in and then like 3 hours later she pulls her car around, comes inside dragging her luggage, puts her keys on the desk and says, 'I need to check out.'

I gave Calvin a look of further confusion and I began to feel even more intrigued.

"What was she doing there?" I asked.

Calvin continued, "Well I asked her if everything was okay. She looked at me confused and asked what I was talking about. I told her that she had only checked in like 3 hours ago and since now she is checking out... I was just wanting to make sure everything was okay and her room was up to par. She said to me, 'I've been in there all night. You checked me in last night.' I tried telling her again that she had only been checked in for 3 hours and she just kept arguing with me and even said, 'I've been in that room all night! You checked me in last night! Why are you hassling me?' It was so weird."

"What in the actual fuck?" Was all I could bring myself to say.

Calvin continued, "Well I told her again that she had been up in her room for only 3 hours and she just asked, 'Well what time is it?' So, I told her it's like a little after 6pm. She thought it was 8 in the morning. She had apparently taken a sleeping pill and thought she had missed her alarm. So hopefully she doesn't like overdose of sleeping pills. She could also be crazy. I don't know."

So, we now have a guest in house who is drugged up and probably insane. At this point I have been around long enough to know this is not just drug induced. This woman had to be crazy and my night could quite possibly turn into a fucking nightmare.

The night went on without police or otherwise emergency services present. For me this was always a nice change of pace. My night seemed to be looking up after all. No word from this woman in 301 either.

Sometime before 6 in the morning, I see a woman come down to the desk with all of her stuff. She walks passed me to the far side of the desk.

Staring straight ahead towards the wall she said, "I need to check out."

I said, "All right. I can get you over here ma'am." Ignoring the fact that she was on the far side of the desk and staring directly at the wall.

She said, "Okay." And continued to stand there and stare off at the wall.

I looked and noticed she not only had the receipt I slipped under the door in hand but it was from room 301. I was hoping I would go my whole shift without being in contact with her.

I told her, "Actually that is your receipt right there for you to keep. So, you are good to go ma'am." I said in hopes of her just leaving with no issue.

She remained in the same place and continued to stare at the wall blankly. Eventually said, "I am actually going to need to pay cash."

So, my plan to get rid of her immediately obviously fell through.

I told her, "All right. Well I can get you on over here then and get you taken care of."

She said, "Okay." And remained in the same spot staring at the wall blankly for a moment.

I remained silent. Sure there was plenty I could say right then but I wanted to see what she was going to say and/or do out of morbid curiosity.

Shortly thereafter, she walked over to the side of the desk I was standing at. I pull up her reservation, she paid in cash, and I handed her change. The fact that this was straight business with no issue getting payment from her gave me some glimmer of hope, and besides the next logical thing for her to do would be to leave.

She then asked, "Is there coffee over there?" Pointing towards the breakfast bar area.

I said, "Yes of course." And she made her way over towards the coffee.

That was when this woman began to act strange and I found myself questioning if I was actually seeing what I was about to see.

I see this woman take a cup off the stack, place it under the coffee carafe, and then just stand there and stare at it for a moment.

I had to wonder what in the hell she was doing.

She then takes this cup, completely empty mind you, and begins to drink it as though this cup had something (such as coffee) in it. She just started drinking a cup of nothing.

Was I seeing this?

I kept watching her. She sat down at a table and stared across from her as though someone was sitting right in front of her. And she continued to drink her cup of nothing.

Was I honestly seeing this? Why was she doing this? Is she crazy?

I tried to make it look like I was doing real actual work to avoid drawing attention to myself as I watched this woman drink her cup of nothing.

After a while she got up carrying her cup of nothing and placed a tea bag in this empty cup of hers. Pretended to steep her tea. Then continued to drink her cup of nothing except now with a tea bag in it. Eventually going to the trash to discard her tea bag but to continue to drink her cup of nothing.

I was considering running over and grabbing her cup of nothing out of her hands and throwing said nothing in her face before yelling something at her about how I hate her and want her out of my life or something. Just to see how she would react.

It was about this time that my coworker who works in the breakfast bar had arrived at work. Who was at the desk to get her keys to the kitchen area.

This woman walks over and asks where she can get some water. My coworker told her she could get some over at the juice machine, and then walked this woman over there to show her.

She fills one of these little plastic cups with water and sits back down setting her cup of water on the table next to her cup of nothing. Then once again proceeded to pick up and drink her cup of nothing all the while a cup of water was sitting on the table.

My coworker was in the kitchen area getting everything ready. I really wanted to run back there to have a second person give me a visual confirmation on what I was witnessing. I couldn't though without drawing attention to myself which may end what was going on and I had to keep watch. I just had to know what she was going to do next.

She kept sitting there wide-eyed drinking her cup of nothing. Was this happening? What was she doing? Why was she doing this? This whole situation becoming as philosophical as it was confusing.

After a bit she stood up, takes her cup of water she never drank, and throws it in the trash. Then she took her cup of nothing and dumped at least 10 creamers into it before putting a tiny little bit of coffee in there and put a lid on it. I guess she finally decided she wanted some coffee with her creamer. Makes sense in a way. I cannot imagine that nothing is very thirst quenching or satiating.

She grabbed her luggage and began to make her way to the back door. I rushed over to the security camera monitor to watch because I just had to know.

I see her dragging her luggage in one hand and carrying her cup in the hand holding it above her head as she prancersized her way out the back door and into legend.

Just entertainment value I do hope to see her again. However, with that level of crazy it is possible she died or something.

AND FOR MY FINAL CHAPTER

Well I'm not dead yet. So, I guess there is something positive in all of this.

As I continue in my misadventures both in and out of the hospitality world, I can only wonder what hell awaits me next.

Maybe I will meet a troll. Like meet a real troll. The kind that you find living under bridges who tries to extort money from goats. I can't imagine that this is very lucrative. Probably why the fucker lives under a bridge. Such a thought as meeting a troll is not all that far-fetched when you think about it. I mean... Some of the guests who have come through may have been such a being, and in the case of some of them, being a troll may be a step up in their existence.

I guess if I had a final message to leave with you is that please remember that the individuals you meet in the industry of hospitality are people too. We have jobs, families, hobbies, hopes and dreams like all of you.

So, take note of that when you are dealing with us. We have jobs where we put up with constant shit from people (in some cases literally shit). So be nice to us because while we won't do anything to jeopardize our jobs; it does not mean we will not find other ways to screw with you. Like putting you in a room near the ice machine or the elevator or by screaming kids. Or if I am feeling particularly devious I may "accidentally" put in a 3 A.M. wake up call to your room, or I may just write an entire book about how insane you all are and how much I have come to loathe your existence.

Just to be clear, I am in no way suggesting with this book that anyone should kill John Lennon, and for what it is worth Jodie Foster will never love you.

Printed and bound by PG in the USA